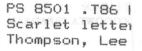
Additional volumes are available.

Scarlet Letters:
MARGARET ATWOOD'S

The Handmaid's Tale

Lee Briscoe Thompson

E C W   P R E S S

THE CANADA COUNCIL | LE CONSEIL DES ARTS
FOR THE ARTS | DU CANADA
SINCE 1957 | DEPUIS 1957

We acknowledge the support of the Canada
Council for the Arts in our publishing program.

This book has been published with the assistance
of a grant from the Ontario Arts Council.

CANADIAN CATALOGUING IN PUBLICATION DATA

Thompson, Lee Briscoe
Scarlet Letters: Margaret Atwood's The handmaid's tale

(Canadian fiction studies ; 34)
Includes bibliographical references and index.
ISBN 1-55022-309-7

1. Atwood, Margaret, 1939– . The handmaid's tale.
I. Title. II. Series.

PS8501.T86H3537 1997   C813'.54   C97-930389-3
PR9199.3.A88H3537 1997

The cover features a reproduction of the
dust-wrapper from the first edition of
The Handmaid's Tale, courtesy The Thomas Fisher
Rare Books Library, University of Toronto.
Frontispiece photograph courtesy Canapress Archives.

Design and imaging by ECW Type & Art, Oakville, Ontario.
Printed by AGMV l'Imprimeur, Cap-Saint-Ignace, Quebec.

Distributed by General Distribution Services,
30 Lesmill Road, Don Mills, Ontario M3B 2T6.

Published by ECW PRESS,
2120 Queen Street East,
Toronto, Ontario M4E 1E2.

http://www.ecw.ca/press

PRINTED AND BOUND IN CANADA

Table of Contents

A Note on the Author

Born in Montreal, Lee Briscoe Thompson grew up there and in Quebec City. She moved to Winnipeg for eight years, completing an honours English degree at the University of Winnipeg and an M.A. at the University of Manitoba, before returning east to complete a Ph.D. at Queen's University, Kingston. After an interim year in Montreal, she joined the faculty of the University of Vermont, teaching in the English Department and the Canadian Studies Program. First as managing editor, then as editor-in-chief, she served the *American Review of Canadian Studies* from 1976 through 1993, and has been a member of several other journal editorial boards. She has published articles and reviews primarily on Canadian literature but also on Australian, New Zealand, and British writers, and has given conference papers and lectures on Canadian and Commonwealth literature in Canada, the United States, Europe, Asia, India, and the South Pacific. In 1987 she published *Dorothy Livesay*, the first full-length study of the Canadian poet.

REFERENCES AND ACKNOWLEDGEMENTS

The text of *The Handmaid's Tale* used in this study is the McClelland and Stewart-Bantam Limited paperback Seal Books edition, published in September 1986. Page references to this edition are given after quotations.

I would like to thank the Canadian Embassy in the United States for a Senior Fellowship and the University of Vermont for a Summer Research Fellowship; both awards assisted substantially in the preparation of this commentary. I also appreciate the intellectual support of my colleagues in the Department of English and the Canadian Studies Program at the University of Vermont, and am indebted to the Interlibrary Loan staff of Bailey-Howe Library for frequent assistance, as well as Marie McGarry for meticulous bibliographic searches and perceptive comments. To Robert Lecker, who has been infinitely patient and supportive, I would like to express my appreciation. Special thanks go also to Judith McCombs for generously opening her home and immense Atwood resources to me, to Nathalie Cooke for kindly reviewing the Chronology, and to anonymous external readers for helpful criticisms. My parents, who did not live to see this publication but never doubted its completion, are also in my thoughts. And I am grateful as always to family and friends for once again standing by.

Scarlet Letters:
Margaret Atwood's
The Handmaid's Tale

Chronology

1939   Margaret Eleanor Atwood born 18 November in Ottawa, Ontario, to Margaret Dorothy Atwood (née Killam) and Carl Edmund Atwood; siblings Harold (b. 1937) and Ruth (b. 1951).

1940–52 Family moves to Sault Ste. Marie (1945), then to Toronto (1946); much of each year is spent in the bush country of Quebec and Ontario, due to father's career as an entomologist.

1952–57 Attends Leaside High School, Toronto; begins writing seriously at sixteen.

1957–61 Attends Victoria College, University of Toronto; graduates with Bachelor of Arts, honours English.

1961   Publishes *Double Persephone* (poetry), which wins the E.J. Pratt Medal. Wins Woodrow Wilson Fellowship to Radcliffe College.

1962   Receives an M.A. from Radcliffe College; continues graduate study at Radcliffe, which merges with Harvard University that year.

1963   Returns to Toronto to work in market research. Drafts a novella (still unpublished), entitled "Up in the Air So Blue."

1964–65 Moves to Vancouver to lecture in English at the University of British Columbia. Drafts novel, *The Edible Woman*, not published until 1969.

1965–67 Returns to Harvard to continue doctoral work on H. Rider Haggard and English metaphysical romance; does not complete degree.

1966   Publishes *The Circle Game*, which wins 1967 Governor General's Award for Poetry.

9

1967	Marries James Polk, an American she met in 1963 at Harvard. Begins teaching Victorian and American literature at Sir George Williams (now Concordia University), Montreal.
1968	Publishes *The Animals in That Country*, which has won First Prize in the 1967 Centennial Commission Poetry Competition.
1969	Moves to Edmonton to begin a year of teaching at the University of Alberta. Publishes *The Edible Woman*.
1970	Two poetry collections, *The Journals of Susanna Moodie* and *Procedures for Underground*; five *Procedures* poems win Union Poetry Prize from *Poetry* (Chicago). Spends most of year in France.
1971	*Power Politics* (poetry). Begins one year of teaching at York University, Toronto. Joins editorial board of House of Anansi Press.
1972	*Surfacing* (novel) and *Survival: A Thematic Guide to Canadian Literature* (criticism). Begins a year as writer-in-residence at University of Toronto.
1973	Moves to Alliston, Ontario, with novelist Graeme Gibson. Receives from Trent University (Peterborough, Ontario) the first of many honorary degrees; becomes a director of Canadian Civil Liberties Union. Resigns from Anansi Press. Becomes involved in Writers' Union of Canada.
1974	*You Are Happy*; several of its poems win Bess Hopkins Prize from *Poetry* (Chicago).
1976	*Lady Oracle* (novel), which wins 1977 City of Toronto Book Award and Canadian Booksellers Association Award, and *Selected Poems*. Gives birth to Eleanor Jess.
1977	*Dancing Girls* (short stories), which wins St. Lawrence Medal and Periodical Distributors of Canada Award for Short Fiction, and *Days of the Rebels: 1815–1840* (Canadian history).
1978	*Two-Headed Poems* and *Up in the Tree* (children's fiction). Travels widely, from Australia to Afghanistan; lives in Edinburgh, Scotland. Farm at Alliston remains home base. Travels extensively hereafter.

1979   *Life before Man* (novel).

1980   *Anna's Pet* (children's fiction) with Joyce Barkhouse. Radcliffe Graduate Society Medal. Moves to Toronto. Vice-president of Writers' Union of Canada.

1981   *True Stories* (poetry) and *Bodily Harm* (novel). Molson Award, Guggenheim Fellowship, Companion of the Order of Canada. First gleam of idea for *The Handmaid's Tale* at a dinner party.

1982   *Second Words: Collected Critical Prose*; edits *The New Oxford Book of Canadian Verse in English*. Welsh Arts Council International Writers Prize. President of Writers' Union of Canada 1982–83.

1983   *Murder in the Dark: Short Fictions and Prose Poems* and *Bluebeard's Egg* (short fiction). Six months' residence in Norfolk, England.

1984   *Interlunar* (poetry). Three months in Berlin on German government writer's grant. Begins writing *The Handmaid's Tale* (novel).

1984–86 President of PEN International, Canadian Centre, Anglophone.

1985   *The Handmaid's Tale*, which wins 1986 Governor General's Award for Fiction, Arthur C. Clarke science fiction award, 1986 Toronto Arts Award, *Los Angeles Times* Award, and place on shortlist for England's Booker Prize. Accepts endowed chair in creative writing, University of Alabama; teaches course on Ontario Gothic literature.

1986   *Selected Poems II: Poems Selected and New, 1976–1986*; co-edits, with Robert Weaver, *The Oxford Book of Canadian Short Stories in English*. Ida Nudel Humanitarian Award of the Canadian Jewish Congress. New York University Berg Chair for three months. British, American, Finnish, and Swedish editions of *Handmaid's Tale* published, as are first Canadian and American paperbacks.

1987   Edits *The Canlit Foodbook*. Fellow, Royal Society of Canada; Woman of the Year, *Ms.* magazine; Humanist of the Year, American Humanist Society. Writer-in-residence, Macquarie University, Sydney, Australia. Norwegian edition of *Handmaid's Tale* published.

1988	*Cat's Eye* (novel), short-listed for Booker Prize, wins Canadian Club Arts and Letters Award plus Book-of-the-Year Award of the Foundation for the Advancement of Canadian Letters; introduction to *Cambridge Guide to Literature in English*. Foreign Honorary Member, Literature, of American Academy of Arts and Sciences.
1989	Author of the Year, Canadian Booksellers Association.
1990	*Selected Poems: 1966–1984* and *For the Birds* (children's fiction). Film version of *Handmaid's Tale* debuts, with script by Harold Pinter, consulting with Atwood. Order of Ontario and Harvard Centennial Medal.
1991	*Wilderness Tips* (short fiction), which wins Trillium Book Award for Excellence in Ontario Writing.
1992	*Good Bones* (short fiction). Co-edits, with Barry Callaghan, and introduces *The Poetry of Gwendolyn MacEwen, Vol. One: The Early Years*.
1993	*The Robber Bride* (novel), which wins Trillium Book Award, Canadian Authors Association Novel of the Year Award; *Good Bones and Simple Murders* (short fictions, prose poems, drawn from *Good Bones* and *Murder in the Dark*, plus one new piece, "Simple Murders"). Co-edits, with Barry Callaghan, *The Poetry of Gwendolyn MacEwen, Vol. Two: The Later Years*. Chevalier des Arts et Lettres (Government of France).
1995	*Morning in the Burned House* (poetry), *Strange Things: The Malevolent North in Canadian Literature* (criticism).
1996	*Alias Grace* (novel), short-listed for Booker Prize, wins Giller Prize.

The Importance of the Work

One way to discuss the importance of *The Handmaid's Tale* is to consider its public impact, which has been enormous throughout North America. In Canada, there were so many advance orders for the latest product of the nation's hottest author that the book went into a second printing a week ahead of its Canadian publication date in 1985. That the novel was about the United States, obsessive subject of most of Canada's cultural, political, and economic ruminations, certainly added to the anticipation. Nor was the approval a merely trendy and temporary phenomenon: a poll of *Books in Canada* readers five years later announced that "The award for the favourite book of the last 10 years was easily won by Margaret Atwood's *The Handmaid's Tale*, which garnered twice as many votes" as did the first runner-up ("Questionnaire Results").

Outside of Canada, while Atwood's writing had always had a coterie of non-Canadian devotees, her audience had been somewhat restricted to serious readers of contemporary literature (above all, fiction) and especially women's writing. For Atwood *The Handmaid's Tale* was, in booksellers' terminology, a "breakthrough" into larger reading markets, a popular success that made Atwood, in a word, famous. Almost instantly, Atwood began appearing in newspapers, on the covers of newsmagazines, in television and radio interviews. *The Handmaid's Tale* was the first book by Atwood to reach the best-seller charts in the United States, and it appeared on all the lists within two weeks of its American publication in February of 1986. Fifteen weeks on the 1986 *New York Times Book Review* best-sellers list in hardcover, *The Handmaid's Tale* encountered a second wave of welcome when it emerged in paperback, spending eight more weeks on the 1987 lists, and a further four weeks in 1990 after the film version inspired a new rush of sales.

The Handmaid's Tale is a novel that transcends particularized tastes and training, that speaks not only to a spectrum of professionals but also to the average person, that comfortably claims a place both in elegant bookshops and on supermarket checkout reading racks. Within the academic community it has gone well beyond the predictable audience of English teachers in attracting the interest of historians, political scientists, sociologists, philosophers, economists, and professors of religion, women's studies, business, and law, finding its way into syllabi in all of those disciplines. *The Handmaid's Tale* has been translated into Danish, Dutch, Finnish, French, German, Italian, Japanese, Korean, Norwegian, Polish, Portuguese, Serbo-Croatian, Slovenian, Spanish, and Swedish, and has been distributed globally. As I shall elaborate in my discussion of the critical reception of the text, no Atwood novel has been as frequently reviewed in the popular press, glossy magazines, *and* scholarly journals as *The Handmaid's Tale*. It is in that combination of popular and academic success that *The Handmaid's Tale* arguably surpasses the acclaim of any previous Canadian novel.

The importance of a book can also be measured by looking at its place within an author's entire canon or body of work. *The Handmaid's Tale* was Atwood's sixth published novel, and to most readers it seemed at first a dramatic departure from her earlier writing strategies: set in the future, cast outside of Canada, moving into the traditionally male domain of anti-utopia or dystopia (Aldous Huxley, Eugene Zamiatin, George Orwell, Anthony Burgess), stepping up the technological level of the orthodox letter/diary form to transcripts from audiocassette tapes, and providing an elaborate epilogue or afternote to the text in a different voice, time, and place. But, upon reflection, readers familiar with Atwood's prose and poetry have come to stress the connections and continuities with her previous (and subsequent) work: the delivery of a commentary that is, in Cathy Davidson's memorable phrase, "both present and tense" (24); the many dualities, structural, stylistic, philosophical, and metaphorical; the razor-sharp descriptions and characterizations, the satire and wordplay, the recurrent image patterns of mirrors, prisons, nature, body parts, colour, light, and dark; the didactic impulse but also the instinct for ambiguity; the ironies and epiphanies of female experience and male-female relations; and the trademark elements of costume gothic, fairytale, and romance.

Judith McCombs, in her "Literary Introduction" to the massive 1991 Atwood bibliography, identifies several discernible stages in Atwood's development as a writer:

> ... an apprentice, allegorical period; the first creative stage, of gothic realism, that extends from the 1966 *Circle Game* to the 1977 *Dancing Girls*; and the second creative stage, of political and didactic realism, that extends from the 1978 *Two-Headed Poems* through at least the 1984 *Interlunar* poems and the 1985 *Handmaid's Tale*; note that the 1990 *Selected Poems 1966–1984* stops with the *Interlunar* poems. The post-*Interlunar* poems, which appear in the 1986 Canadian *Selected Poems II: Poems Selected and New*, and the kindred 1988 *Cat's Eye*, with its mystic realism and its portrait of the aging artist in Toronto, may well begin a third parallel and mirroring creative stage; in which, one predicts, Atwood's image-laden, resonant, collage- and mirror-structured fiction will increasingly be called postmodern, and may continue to incorporate more and more of what became lyric poetry in the first creative stage. (xii–xiii)

Certainly the attention to precise and vicious realities of political tyranny and torture incline one to group *The Handmaid's Tale* in terms of content with *Bodily Harm*, *True Stories*, and *Two-Headed Poems*, although less so with *Interlunar* and *Murder in the Dark*. Given the quasi-autobiographical turn of her next novel, *Cat's Eye*, the return to private lives in her subsequent collection of short stories, *Wilderness Tips*, and novel, *The Robber Bride*, the largely personal intensity of her new poems, *Morning in the Burned House*, and the biographical case-history approach of her new novel, *Alias Grace*, it may not be too soon to group *The Handmaid's Tale*, as McCombs does, with a more overtly politicized phase in Atwood's career, and to see that novel as a sort of culmination, her strongest political vision to date.

Beyond the public response and the book's status within the author's canon, there is a third gauge, more meaningful, of the importance of a work: its literary accomplishment and artistic quality. For validation of *The Handmaid's Tale* on that score, one might first point to its winning Canada's highest literary distinction, the 1986 Governor General's Award for Fiction, joining the Governor

General's Award for Poetry that Atwood had won nearly twenty years earlier for *The Circle Game*. Ultimately, however, the best way to test the calibre of *The Handmaid's Tale* is in a close reading of the text.

Critical Reception

By the mid 1980s Margaret Atwood was already, despite her grumbles to the contrary, a lionized figure in Canada. But with *The Handmaid's Tale*, she finally caught the U.S. imagination, and her popular appeal has been fully reflected in the large number of book reviews, articles, and academic theses that appeared, and continue to appear over a decade later. For the first time in Atwood's career, the number of U.S. reviews dramatically outstripped the number in Canada (McCombs xviii). It almost seemed that every newspaper, magazine, and journal in the United States felt compelled to react to Atwood's provocative scenario, from the *Washington Post* to the *Kalamazoo Gazette*, from the *American Atheist* to the *Christian Century*, from the *Wall Street Journal* to *Glamour*.

Shrewd timing appears to have been a factor in the extraordinary flood of interest. *The Handmaid's Tale* arrived on the scene in the U.S. at a time of growing alarm in many quarters. The radical right believed a permissive minority was demolishing the rules and customs that had made America great; they saw "a society dying," as the novel's Aunt Lydia puts it at the Red Centre, "of too much choice" (24). The radical left felt it was witnessing a creeping cancellation of the legislative gains of the 1960s and 1970s — civil, labour, reproductive, environmental, and other protections — due to conservative regimes responding to a right-wing fringe and exploiting the fears of an uninformed middle class. The great majority in the middle were being bombarded to an unprecedented degree by media accounts of the failings and disasters of post-Watergate, post-Vietnam America. Almost nobody was impervious to some vision of sweeping change and extreme solutions.

Atwood commented in the *Washington Post* that

The question they always ask in Canada [about *The Handmaid's Tale*] is, 'Could it happen here?' . . . Whereas in the States they're saying, 'Boy, this could really happen here.' Maybe not my exact scenario, which has elements of satire in it, but some of the underpinnings are certainly in the air in this country. (Battiata G6)

Conceding to Larry Black in the *Vancouver Sun* that not all Americans think Gilead could happen in the U.S., Atwood explained that those who deny the possibility have forgotten that the United States "didn't start out as a liberal democracy. . . . It started out as a Puritan colony that expelled, hung and burned heretics."

The novel has attracted a huge amount of attention through its dystopian strategy of drawing upon a recognizable present to create its nightmarish future. Offred's reminiscences about her pre-Gilead life and her allusions (so humanly faulty) to history before her lifetime give the reader the factual linkages necessary for an emotional and intellectual attachment to the novel. Lest we miss or resist that historical connection, Atwood has the Commander, the Aunts, the Marthas, Offred, and Moira all discuss it at one point or another. And Professor Pieixoto scrutinizes closely the historical antecedents of Gilead that lead him inexorably to the conclusion that "there was little that was truly original with or indigenous to Gilead: its genius was synthesis" (289). Atwood has reiterated this point time and again, defending her novel against charges of implausibility by arguing that nothing in Gilead is wildly fanciful or unprecedented historically: "There is nothing in this book that hasn't already happened in the past, including the United States or European past, or isn't already happening somewhere else in the world" (Matheson 20). In early interviews Atwood believed there was one exception, the funeral for a fetus (42), but later received confirmation that even that had happened. "I was quite careful about [not inventing]. . . . I transposed to a different time and place, but the motifs are all historical motifs" (Cathy Davidson 24).

Surveying 116 U.S. book reviews of *The Handmaid's Tale*, and comparing them with 52 from Canada, 26 from the United Kingdom, and 16 from other European or Commonwealth countries (Australia, New Zealand, India, France, Spain, Germany, and Finland), has been instructive. Predictably, in Canada and the States roughly

18

two-thirds of the reviewers were female, doubtless because many editors-in-chief automatically placed a "feminist" novel in the hands of women. Tallying the number of *women* reviewers who expressed a positive overall view of the novel, I discovered — perhaps again predictably — that the vast majority approved of Atwood's performance: 93 percent in the U.S., 96 percent in Canada, with only a moderate drop-off in the U.K. (80 percent) and the other countries (77 percent). More interesting was the comparison of those results with the positions of *male* reviewers: only 59 percent of the Americans gave a positive final assessment of the novel, joined by 57 percent of the British and 74 percent of the Canadian men. (Atwood pleased 75 percent of the men outside the North Atlantic triangle, but it should be remembered that we are canvassing only four people there.) So men, in general, responded to *The Handmaid's Tale* with less enthusiasm than did women.

Although Atwood's style and the nationality of the reviewer enter the equation in explaining this gender gap in approval ratings, it seems above all to be connected with the perceived credibility of the novel. "Credible" does not mean that the tale is prophetic, that Gilead is about to heave into view; it just allows that it *could* happen and that the novel operates as a believable cautionary tale clearly rooted in the nature of our own times. Utopias imagine positive future societies which will have solved the problems of our current flawed world, while dystopias extend certain negative contemporary conditions to even grimmer future extremes. In either mode, the reader obviously must see clearly the connection between present reality and fictional future if the vision is to have power and point. This means that literary critics considering a dystopic novel such as *The Handmaid's Tale* must pay attention to an issue they might entirely ignore in discussing another type of fiction: believability. And critics did so, often hotly, occasionally obsessively.

Only half of the U.S. male reviewers found the scenario plausible, as opposed to 76 percent of American women. North of the border the proportion of Canadian men who found Gilead credible was higher (60 percent), but so was the female yea (94 percent). Intriguingly, only 43 percent of British males thought the situation possible, while their female counterparts were 93 percent convinced. In the other countries tabulated, fully 75 percent of the men considered the situation believable and 100 percent of the women agreed. Atwood's vision, Offred's testimony, and the plodding prisoner's pace at which they are delivered evidently struck women in a positive way that was not overwhelmed by other considerations, such as the sketchiness of socioeconomic and governmental details, which so bothered or bored a sizeable minority of male critics. Two famous exceptions to this gender generalization are American novelists Mary McCarthy and John Updike: she rejected it, he admired it.

In impromptu surveys of eight classes of American university students with whom I've discussed the novel, I can add the unscientific unisex data that only 6 percent have scoffed at the premise of *The Handmaid's Tale* and that the percentage of sceptics dropped between 1987 and 1995, as television evangelism, surrogate motherhood, nuclear accidents, ethnic cleansing, and other news items provided living illustrations for aspects of Atwood's fiction. Even remarkable developments toward freedom — the fall of the Berlin Wall, the dissolution of the USSR, the crumbling of South African apartheid, etc. — appeared to occur with such stunning speed as to confirm the feasibility of Atwood's vision of a sudden coup, a rapid social reversal.

Another reason for the strength of response to this particular Atwood novel has to do, I think, with the protagonist. Reviewers have reacted variously to Offred, but almost always with considerable energy. Whether they praise her courage or denounce her wimpishness, celebrate her understatement or deplore her monotone, most readers feel they have met a "real" character in a genuinely terrifying situation, and they more often than not come to care as she struggles for mental, physical, emotional, and ethical survival. Previous Atwood fiction seemed to favour one or the other of two female heads: an apparently brittle, bored, and self-absorbed narrative voice which emerged from the mouth of an independent professional of the Me Generation (see *Life before Man, Bodily Harm*, etc.); or, alternately, an intellectually lightweight pop-cultural voice which some readers thought condescending or to which they themselves had a condescending attitude (see *Lady Oracle*, "Rape Fantasies" from *Dancing Girls*, etc.). In *The Handmaid's Tale* Atwood seems to merge those two voices, so that Offred speaks, as it were, two-headedly (or, to use the Canadian idiom, bilingually). And in the crucible of social oppression, the fusion not only works but commends the protagonist to the reader in a powerful new way.

Atwood's immediately previous novel, *Bodily Harm*, does present a situation of brutal oppression, but situates it at some remove from mainstream North America (on a Caribbean island) where Rennie is a tourist visitor to the repressive social scene but not an integral part of it; in *The Handmaid's Tale*, by contrast, Offred is the centrepiece of the state's, her state's, oppression. The merging of those two Atwood voices in a non-touristic, full-time, life-and-death situation seems to have broadened the protagonist's appeal and to have earned Offred a level of compassionate respect often withheld from previous Atwood female leads.

The Handmaid's Tale, like all art, is as much a Rorschach test for the reader/reviewer as it is a freestanding entity. What we see in it is heavily determined by who we are, how we see the world, what we value. Gender, political positioning, age, nationality, personal experience, degree and type of literary education are only a few of the crucial factors in what we choose to emphasize, ignore, praise, or denounce in a reading of this or any other text. And it is even more the case when we face a text that calls upon us to participate, that teases us into detective work on the plot, that engages our emotions, opinions, and preconceptions so immediately. It is not surprising, then, that critical reaction to *The Handmaid's Tale* has been so extremely lively and contradictory. Scarcely a reading of character, plot, setting, genre, imagery, or authorial intention has been proposed by one critic that has not been vigorously rejected by another, often in tones of dismay or amused contempt.

After the frenzy of book reviews in 1985 and 1986, critical commentary on *The Handmaid's Tale* settled down to the more leisurely pace of articles, anthology contributions, master's theses, and doctoral dissertations. Nearly one hundred of these have appeared over the last ten years, with the numbers peaking in 1989–90. From the beginning *The Handmaid's Tale* has attracted academics from a long list of disciplines, such as law, bioethics, politics, social theory, philosophy, communications, and environmental studies; some come to the novel primarily for segments of the text that address their extraliterary mission (e.g., Armbruster, Culp, McKie), while others linger in richly interdisciplinary inquiries (e.g., Bergmann, Burack, Gotsch-Thomson, Langer, St. Peter). The book has also been particularly useful to scholars in the intersection of theological and women's studies (see Filipczak, Kaler, Larson, Mollenkott, Workman). And it has also become fashionable to refer to the novel in aid of issues ranging from labour legislation to child adoption.

In literary studies *The Handmaid's Tale* is often compared and contrasted with other texts. At first the pairings tended to be with male writers' dystopian classics (Huxley's *Brave New World*, Orwell's *Nineteen Eighty-Four*, Zamiatin's *We*, Bradbury's *Fahrenheit 451*, Burgess's *A Clockwork Orange*, etc.), and with Marge Piercy's female utopia in *Woman on the Edge of Time*. More recently it has been linked frequently with women's fictional narratives by the likes of Margaret Drabble, Faye Weldon, Nora Ephron, Virginia Woolf, Toni Morrison, and Alice Walker. When the novel is treated on its own, commentary has most often focused on culture and feminist politics, and considerable energy has gone into genre discussions of *The Handmaid's Tale* as a "dystopia," "feminist dystopia," "contextual dystopia," "speculative fiction," "comedy of manners in a Gothic-dystopia," and other distinctions. (See, for example, articles by Banerjee, Caldwell, Deer, Nischik, and Wood on the novel as a dystopia; by Baccolini, Bartkowski, Bazin, Ferns, Fitting, Malak, Murphy, Sauterbailliet, and Stein re feminist dystopia.) Critical attention to matters of female voice, narratology, and fictional autobiography stand next in frequency (see Bouson, Buss, Conboy, Nathalie Cooke, Freibert, Garrett-Petts, Givner, Hammer, Kauffman, and Kolodny). Language has been the central consideration of essays by Michèle Lacombe, Harriet Bergmann, Jeanne Campbell Reesman, and Debrah Raschke, and imagery, important in many articles, has been especially foregrounded by Dorothy Jones and Constance Rooke. Several critics have broken ground on special aspects of the text: Roberta Rubenstein on "Nature and Nurture," Sandra Tomc on nationalism, Susanna Finnell on the quest myth, Sharon Wilson on fairy tale, A.R. Kizuk on psychology, Martin Kuester on parodic structures, and Mark Evans on the dedicatees to the novel. Madonne Miner has engaged in a lively challenge to Coral Ann Howells, Barbara Ehrenreich, Amin Malak, and Victoria Glendinning about their view of love as a revolutionary force in the novel, and Joseph Andriano has contributed a fascinating argument that the game of Scrabble is a trope for the entire novel. The "Historical Notes," completely unmentioned in 84 percent of the book reviews, finally have received stimulating and extended inquiry in articles by Arnold E. Davidson, Michael Foley, and Ken Norris (see also

Bergmann, Bouson, Garrett-Petts, Hengen, Kauffman, Malak, and Wilson). Overseas critics are increasingly studying the novel as one of the classics of contemporary fiction, and its canonization in hundreds of Canadian and contemporary literature courses guarantees that its critical reception will be an unfinished tale for a considerable time to come.

Reading of the Text

INTRODUCTION

In 1983, with twenty-three volumes of poetry, fiction, and literary criticism to her credit, Atwood launched into a new novel during a six-month stay in England. But an idea that had been lurking at the back of her head for a few years kept interrupting, "getting in the way and clamoring for attention" (Adachi). Atwood resisted and soldiered on with the other project until early 1984, convinced that she would be denounced as paranoid and extremist if she were to produce the seemingly "crazed and berserk" tale ("Q&Q Interview" 66). But the voice became too insistent, and she found herself beginning to accumulate a file of news clippings related to the topic: for instance, compulsory testing in Romanian factories to detect pregnancies and abortions; a fundamentalist sect in New Jersey which referred to women as handmaidens; declining fertility in European countries (Dudar).

Then, winning an artist's grant to write in Germany for three months, unencumbered by any lecturing or mentoring responsibilities, gave Atwood the leisure to begin the risky manuscript. In Berlin from March through May of 1984 she wrote quickly, and later she was able to complete revisions of *The Handmaid's Tale* while holding an endowed chair at the University of Alabama in early 1985. It is interesting to reflect on the remarkable suitability of the locations in which she was working on that dark novel: the city of the Berlin Wall, entrenched symbol of totalitarian repression, and the American Deep South, a region historically associated with slavery and Protestant fundamentalism.

If the advisability of writing such a controversial novel was uncertain to begin with, its setting was not. Atwood had no doubts that the United States and specifically Cambridge, Massachusetts, were the right choices. Canada would not serve her purposes, she has explained, because of its innate conservatism and because half of its population was Roman Catholic. It fit popular stereotypes *and* historical precedent for Canada in *The Handmaid's Tale* to peer down anxiously at America's muscular social experiment and, as in the American Revolution, the slavery era, and the Vietnam years, to offer sanctuary but try not to outrage American authorities. Arguably for the better more than the worse, Canada had never had Manifest Destiny, a Committee for un-Canadian Activities, a Civil War, a Revolution, or a Puritan monotheocracy. As Atwood put it, "The water doesn't all wash to one side of the bathtub in the way it does in the States. The States tends to go in swings that are a lot more extreme than ours" (qtd. in Goddard 8). The United States made a much more believable setting, with its history as well as its reputation for change, action, and missionary conviction.

Further, Atwood's own ancestors were New England Puritans, immigrants from England in the 1630s who had moved on to Nova Scotia during the United Empire Loyalist exodus provoked by the American Revolution. In shifting from Toronto to the United States to pursue graduate study, Atwood in part had been intent upon learning more about those forebears, about American Puritanism, and about the only large-scale theocracy North America has ever known. In consequence of a total of four years at Radcliffe and Harvard, Atwood had acquired an intimate knowledge of Cambridge, a physical familiarity crucial to her technique of sharply etched, accurate descriptive detail. And Cambridge was an especially appropriate venue in a variety of other respects: with Harvard's reputation as a centre of intellectual freedom to play off against Gilead's lethal anti-intellectualism; with the modest size of the community lending itself to a vision of social control more than would some large and sprawling city; with the geographical configuration of Cambridge as a militarily defensible "island" marked off from Boston by the Charles River, with sea access; and with an actual brick wall around Harvard Yard to exploit concretely, symbolically, and ironically in her narrative.

Other forces facilitated the writing of *The Handmaid's Tale*. Atwood, after an early reticence about overt involvement in politics, had come to appreciate that politics is everpresent, that all of life is in some sense political. By the 1980s she was active in a number of organizations ranging from the Writers' Union of Canada to PEN International, a writers' group with a particular concern about imprisoned and oppressed writers around the world. She had travelled extensively in countries with repressive regimes, such as Iran and Afghanistan, and had followed current events closely enough to be deeply conscious of how quickly power could shift within a state. Her reading ranged widely in histories of World War II, totalitarianism, sociobiological theory, and Amnesty International accounts of human rights violations from South America through Asia. And, versed in the literary traditions of utopia and dystopia, Atwood had already introduced a strong political voice into her poetry, fiction, and essays. In *True Stories* Atwood had anticipated Gilead in writing poems about (and themselves like)

> a flayed body untangled
> string by string and hung
> to the wall, an agonized banner
> displayed for the same reason
> flags are. ("Torture" 51)

In *Bodily Harm* the action was brought nearer to home in the sense that it indicted those who try to stay apolitical, who think themselves detached from the dirty fray of power politics, the case in point being those "sweet Canadians" (*Bodily Harm* 135) who protect themselves from harsh global realities.

An intersection between institutional and gender politics, *The Handmaid's Tale* was also inspired by a long list of contemporary developments. They included the failure of the Equal Rights Amendment in the United States; the rise of a vocally conservative Moral Majority (which liberal bumper stickers argued was neither moral nor a majority); the decline in Caucasian birthrates, combined with an increase in nonwhite immigration and births; survivalist, neo-Nazi, and white-supremacist groups spreading throughout North America; the entry of fundamentalist preachers into politics and into positions of remarkable power and persuasion via television; the early but escalating fears about Acquired Immunodeficiency Syndrome (AIDS); the increasingly vocal calls for free sexual choices (including of course abortion, homosexuality, and complete gender equality) countered by increasingly hostile resistance to those movements, seen as antithetical to "family values." This is simply a partial listing of all the social, sexual, and spiritual anxieties prevalent during the 1970s and 1980s (with no relief in sight as I write this in the mid 1990s). Thus, while the grim scenario of *The Handmaid's Tale* may represent a future response to the trends and developments of what Offred will call "the time before," the novel is itself a brilliantly satiric response to "the time before," a thinly veiled and only mildly exaggerated "now."

There has been a tendency for commentators to speak of the "frame" provided by the "Historical Notes" which follow Offred's narrative. There is an almost visual logic in seeing the personal account as a tight focus from which we cinematically draw back to consider the so-called big picture; the speaker in the epilogue in fact insists on the necessity of seeing this handmaid "within the broad outlines of the moment in history of which she was a part" (287). To conceive of the "Historical Notes" as the frame, however, is to skim over the dedications and epigraphs that precede the opening chapter. Taken together, these elements can be viewed as parentheses, a more inclusive idea which accords much greater status to the rich material at the beginning of *The Handmaid's Tale*.

Often unnoticed by readers plunging into chapter 1 is the simple dedication: "For Mary Webster and Perry Miller." Mary Webster turns out to be an ancestor of Atwood's, one of "those people in the dour, black, strait-laced pictures" ("Q&Q Interview" 67) that Offred will later notice in the home of the Commander and in the chapel/ museum she visits with Ofglen. Accused of witchcraft in the infamous Salem witch trials, Mary Webster was found guilty and hanged. But when she was cut down the following day, she was miraculously still alive, and under the law of double jeopardy had to be set free. It may be from this bizarre incident in her family history that Atwood has acquired a distrust of theocracies, not to mention a predisposition to see women as survivors, a consistent characteristic of her protagonists. She has also, as she has remarked herself, needed Mary's tough neck to stand up to some of the critical reactions to her book.

Perry Miller, the other dedicatee, moves Atwood's interest in the Puritans from the seventeenth century to the twentieth and from the particulars of her personal ancestral past to the generalities of an official historical past. Miller was a prominent and respected scholar at Harvard, with whom Atwood studied early American history and the Puritan church-state. The positive light in which Atwood views this intellectual sets him in counterpoint to his pompous and sexist successor of 2195; while the academic of the future ridicules the quality of a twentieth-century North American college education, it is not clear to the reader whether he and his sort have made much progress over Perry Miller in a couple of centuries. It is also possible that Atwood as former student is offering to the shade of her former professor an angle on the Puritans somewhat neglected in traditional studies of the period: the private, personal, anecdotal experience of a single woman.

After the dedication, a trinity of epigraphs announces *The Handmaid's Tale*: one biblical, one literary, and one proverbial. The first, from Genesis, gives the text that the leaders of Gilead will take as scriptural authorization for the most arcane of their social practices. As the ancient story goes, Rachel, unable to conceive, "gives" her fertile handmaid (maidservant) Bilhah to Rachel's husband, Jacob, so that a child may result. The blessing of divine precedent is thus argued by the self-styled Sons of Jacob in Gilead to justify the system of Handmaids for procreative purposes. What helped to perpetuate the chosen people in biblical times must be reinstated to revitalize God's numbers (read *Caucasian* numbers), driven down by humankind's abuses of His creation. That we know nothing of Bilhah's view of that arrangement reminds us of all the silently exploited and silenced women of history, whose stories hover outside the official version.

The second quotation, from Jonathan Swift's *A Modest Proposal*, is probably equally familiar to the average reader. Swift, an eighteenth-century Anglo-Irish satirist, mocked the British government's repressive policies toward Ireland by offering, in the voice of a naive and well-meaning narrator, a diabolical proposal: reduce the crushing poverty of the Irish by starting up a trade in tasty Irish infant flesh. Impoverished children, the narrator blandly pointed out, would thus provide an urgently needed food source, relieve their families of the burden of their upkeep, spare themselves a life of painful want, and turn a nice profit for their masters. The persuasively genial good will with which this ghastly suggestion was made is the engine of the satiric impact.

In *The Handmaid's Tale*, Atwood imagines a society which more than one reviewer of the novel has termed an "efficient" and arguably logical, although extreme, extension of current social realities. But Gilead, whatever "logic" we may apply, is a nightmare, and there is a curious inversion, an ironic "progress," in the fact that Swift's commodities, babies, become the prize in pursuit of which Gilead's women become commodities over two centuries later. Atwood also reverses Swift's proposition: where he presented a brutal and out-landish solution to a crisis of *over*population, she shows Gilead as a brutal and outlandish solution to a crisis of *under*population. For both authors, however, the victims are either women or children first.

There are also stylistic parallels with *A Modest Proposal* in the low-key, unsensational manner with which Offred describes her situation, especially the impregnation Ceremony and the grisly Par-ticiciution. But, given that Swift's narrator is a male making a horrific social proposal, perhaps a more pertinent parallel is Commander Fred, telling Offred in measured and cordial tones about the reason-ableness of Gilead's social project as a constructive remedy to the problems of the "time before." Still, my vote on the stylistic parallels goes finally to Professor Pieixoto in the "Historical Notes," who speaks in the voice of sweet reason to deliver himself of such hair-raising suggestions as the advisibility of Nick's killing Offred to protect himself. Whichever the application, Swift and Atwood both increase exponentially the impact of their satire through the contrast between the madness of their scenarios and the earnest calm of the narrative voices with which they are delivered.

The third epigraph, a Sufi proverb, is the most difficult to connect with the text or even decipher with assurance. "In the desert there is no sign that says, Thou shalt not eat stones." Almost all commen-tators on *The Handmaid's Tale* have simply ignored this; a rare few have alluded in passing to its bleakness. Lucy Freibert briefly extrapolates from it an expression of confidence in human instincts about things to do and things to avoid, an implied indictment of excessive social control (Gilead), and a plea "for human freedom and survival" (285). The single critic to pay it detailed attention has been Nancy Workman, who suggests that Sufi mysticism is a unifying element in the novel and that Offred represents the Sufi spirit and practice. Sufism, not an organized religion but a very individual approach to the spiritual and the secular, has general characteristics which are echoed in the tale. Offred's "reduced circumstances" (8), for instance, reflect the Sufi principle of asceticism, while her inward and intensely personal quest for values and truth fulfils the Sufi goal of a private and individual apprehension of God and the universe. Offred's tendency to utter proverb-like remarks, to detect complexity in apparent simplicity, and to indulge in wordplay are all Sufi practices. As well, the roles of personal rituals, of night as a profound time of ethical and spiritual quest, and of Offred's breathing exercises (for birth preparation but also to suppress forbidden laughter) all accord with aspects of the Sufi faith. Like contemporary novelist Doris Lessing, Atwood may also be attracted to Sufi traditions for their celebration of female strength and leadership. And one cannot dismiss the possibility that Atwood the trickster enjoys the prospect of baffling literary critics with an enigmatic epigraph outside their comfortably familiar Judeo-Christian range of references.

Even in epigraphs, then, Atwood keeps things open-ended. To do so, as is evident from an examination of the manuscripts and working papers lodged at the University of Toronto, she discarded an interesting assortment of other epigraphs, all considerably more straightforward and didactic than the Sufi proverb. For example, she was tempted by a United Nations report on the status of women:

> ... women represent fifty percent of the adult world population, one third of the official labour force, perform nearly two-thirds of all working hours, receive only one-tenth of world income and own less than one percent of world property. (box 72)

In a similar vein, a quotation from Germaine Greer's *Sex and Destiny* (448) was a candidate briefly:

> ... we must never forget that birth promotion was also vigorously carried out: women were ineluctably drawn into the reproduction process to risk their lives in the service of the group time and again by all the social and ideological pressures that could be mustered to the task.

Atwood also considered but rejected a quotation about the naturalness of polygamy (Lumsden 161). And she tried out but decided against several excerpts from fiction and poetry, concerning variously the relation between declining birthrates and a failure to appreciate maternity, storytelling as a female survival strategy, and forced childbearing followed by forced separation of child from mother. While all of these clearly had direct applications to *The Handmaid's Tale*, Atwood used them more indirectly in the content of the novel and, in deciding on the Sufi saying, made a choice which gave greater range, balance, and ambiguity to her trio of epigraphs.

Oh, yes, what *does* it mean? While your guess is as good as mine, I might paraphrase it as: "In a state of deprivation (desert/Gilead), all rules of normal logic (such as, Don't Eat Stones) are suspended"; or maybe, "In bleak conditions, signposts telling one the obvious are unnecessary"; or, if one assumes a clichéd view of the desert as a place with lots of sand but no stone, there is, "In reduced circumstances, don't worry about resisting what isn't even there." Or how about, "In an Atwood text, there is no sign that says, This is exactly what this means"?

THE LAY OF THE LAND

In the United States of the early twenty-first century, a white, right-wing, theocratic coup has taken place. The elite Sons of Jacob, allegedly alarmed by a decline in Caucasian birthrates and by the degeneration of a "traditional" American society, have ironically used "an obscure 'C.I.A.' pamphlet on the destabilization of foreign governments" (289) to mastermind the murder of the president and a massacre in Congress. Blaming unnamed terrorists and playing upon the public's fears of the numerous escalating social disorders, they create a state of panic which permits "temporary" suspension of the Constitution. Next to vanish is free access to the two major requirements for any resistance to the coup — money and information — and a frightened, confused populace hunkers down to ride out the crisis, to survive the rapid changes in its society.

Swiftly a rigid codification is imposed. Most dramatically and visibly, women are stripped of jobs and financial independence and pressed into one of eight categories. Wives of the elite are permitted to maintain their homes and domestic privileges. Singles, divorcees, widows, and women in holy orders, if still capable of childbearing, are forcibly recruited to become Handmaids, a position geared entirely to the production of babies for the older, often sterile elite. Infertile women sufficiently dedicated to the new regime and possessed of leadership skills may become Aunts, a paramilitary cadre in charge of indoctrinating Handmaids and enforcing female (even Wifely) obedience to the new rules. Other barren women of lesser gifts become household drudges named Marthas, who cook and clean for the elite. Beyond these carefully designated groups are the Econowives, wed to low-ranking men and expected to perform all the traditional female functions: manage households, bear children, cook and scrub. Into a dumping category called Unwomen go all the undesirables: the elderly, the nuns who will not recant their vows, the unrepentant radicals, and the "Gender Traitors" (incorrigible lesbians); fated to work in the so-called Colonies, they will, if lucky, labour as field hands in cotton or other crops, but more likely dispose of bodies after battles, or, fatally, clean up toxic wastes and radiation spills. Some aged Widows have been let be, presumably because of high connections, but their numbers are dwindling fast. And off the official charts altogether are the prostitutes who service the Sons of Jacob and foreign trade delegates: the Jezebels of the new order, mostly subversives and unproductive Handmaids sent to brothels as an alternative to the death-dealing Colonies.

To keep everyone in her place more efficiently, the women of Gilead are literally and simplistically colour-coded. Gowns and veils for the Wives are powder blue — colour of bluebloods, of a blue-ribbon aristocracy, of the asexual Virgin Mary, and of a figure of speech for melancholy. Their daughters, whether biologically theirs or produced by a Handmaid, wear virginal white until married off to deserving members of the military. The Handmaids are clothed in red — colour of blood, of menses, of birth, of scarlet women, passion, and (now officially sanctioned) adultery, of Little Red Riding Hood in a very hostile forest; their nunlike habits are completed by a white headdress with white blinders, a parody of liberating white wings. The Aunts wear army khaki without veils, befitting their quasi-military role, and reminiscent of the fascistic Brownshirts of World War II (not to mention the no less fascistic childhood Brownie troop uniforms of other Atwood fiction!). Dull green suits the Marthas in their tedious service functions of feeding and scrubbing; their occasional voluntary wearing of a veil is an ironic vanity since nobody regards a Martha's face as worth a second glance. The Econowives declare their multifunctionality in their cheap, thin dresses striped in Handmaid red, Wife blue, and Martha green (although conspicuously not Aunt khaki since they have no administrative powers). Unwomen — twenty-five percent of whom are actually gay males — wear long grey dresses, the colour of ashes, while the few remaining tolerated Widows predictably wear black. Jezebels, operating outside the official structure and dress code, sport a bizarre assortment of extremely colourful but frazzled and outdated costumes associated with eroticism: Playboy bunny and cheerleader outfits, baby-doll pyjamas, beach bikinis, showgirl glitter, and sexercise warm-ups. A quick colour inventory tells a Gilead male exactly what to expect from the women he encounters.

While some describe Gilead as a fantasy of male control, the men of Gilead do not escape categorization and strict ranking. At the top, of course, are the black-clad Commanders of the Faith, the Sons of Jacob to whose households the Handmaids are assigned. Beneath the Commanders are the Eyes, the spying and intelligence operatives of the regime, dressed in black or grey suits, often wearing ominous dark glasses and riding in black vans with tinted windows and a white-winged eye motif on the sides. The ladder-rung below is occupied by the black-uniformed Angels of the Apocalypse and Angels of Light, soldiers who may aspire to become bridegrooms to the pale and silent daughters of the elite. Beneath the Angels are the Guardians of the Faith, wearing green uniforms that indicate their approximate equivalence to Marthas; assigned to menial jobs, they are "either stupid or older or disabled or very young, apart from the ones that are Eyes incognito" (20). The lowest echelon of men is the great mass of workers, who go their immemorial way, acquiring Econowives, knowing little about the internal operations of their society, wearing nondescript "civilian suits" (159), keeping their heads down and feeling mostly relief when not arrested in the Kafkaesque atmosphere of Gilead. Outside the pale is a small group of doctors kept on hand for medical emergencies and the checking of Handmaid fertility, physicians who have not been accused of performing abortions in the time before Gilead. And for those who still mistake Gilead for a male sexist paradise, it is worth remembering that most of the bodies hanging from hooks on the Wall are male: abortionists, Catholic priests, false converts from Judaism, Jehovah's Witnesses, members of the resistance, homosexuals (like lesbians, called Gender Traitors), and in the fullness of time and systemic purges, even founder-architects of Gilead.

To achieve this level of social compliance, ongoing mechanisms of repression are required. First, forbid all females — except the Aunts, and they only sparingly — to read or write, and in fact reduce the entire society to a condition of functional illiteracy. Second, declare the practices of your new society to rest upon biblical authority (after all, who's going to argue with God's Word?) and then lock up the Bible to any but the Commanders to prevent research on your dogma. Third, withdraw freedoms from only a few groups at a time, cowing the rest of the citizenry and delaying mass resistance until there is nobody left to protest. Fourth, make punishable any unnecessary communication or exchange of information, using isolation and uncertainty to enforce docility. Fifth, continue to control currency, reducing economic activity to easily monitored computer transactions and the exchange of childlike tokens. Sixth, restrict all freedom of movement with checkpoints, identity tattoos, computer systems, surveillance, spotlights, and patrols. Seventh, use public punishment to keep the population in a constant state of anxiety and defensiveness. Eighth, from the start take control of the media and use them, if at all, to deliver a relentless barrage of propaganda. Ninth, ritualize all details of daily life, to grind out of people's lives the nonconformities and the opportunities for even small choices (and therefore freedom of action and thought, and the retention of individual identity). And finally, sanction only one relationship, that between an individual and the collectivity of the State, and only one identity, the tightly defined role to be played in the new system.

When we enter Gilead, however, it is still in its early stages and the course of true totalitarianism is not running entirely smoothly. The new regime's ruthlessness is failing to quell resistance by groups which range from Quakers to southern Baptists, working underground under the code word "Mayday" as well as engaging in military action from Kentucky to Michigan. A black market exists, and gossip within groups is irrepressible. While the major rules have been established, many secondary ones remain to be devised. As Offred remarks about the convention for which door Handmaids should use to enter Commanders' houses, "Things haven't settled down, it's too soon, everyone is unsure about our exact status. After a while it will be either all front doors or all back" (13). It is a transition generation whose previous ways of life are resistant to erasure. The regime is still ironing out the wrinkles, consolidating its procedures by trial and error, making mistakes that leave gaps into which to slip a Handmaid's tale.

THE TIME BEFORE

The society that preceded Gilead, often referred to as "the time before," is obviously similar to our own. Nuclear plant accidents, leaks from countless legal and illegal toxic waste disposal sites, and the cumulative use of pesticides and other chemicals have contaminated the environment and are blamed for an increase in miscarriages, stillbirths, and genetic deformities. Birth control, abortion, venereal disease including AIDS, and increasing acceptance of same-sex relationships also have contributed to the decline of the Caucasian birthrate. Reproductive technology, which had seemed to promise greater freedoms for women, instead has brought them ominously close to being the "two-legged wombs" (128) to which Offred will feel herself reduced in Gilead.

When violence and murder accelerate, people cope with their rising fears by dissociating themselves from the newpaper stories, dismissing them as "bad dreams dreamt by others" (53). Women have mastered unspoken self-defense procedures and most have accepted as inevitable the encroachments on their mobility and peace of mind. Some activists such as Offred's mother have demonstrated in order to "Take Back the Night," but feminist visibility has provoked a sexist backlast and possibly an escalation of sexual mayhem. Seeking allies anywhere, radical feminists have accepted dangerous bedfellows in uniting with fundamentalists to burn pornography, an early prohibition on reading that will play into the hands of the Sons of Jacob.

Meanwhile, relations between men and women are, in Commander Fred's term from the old days, a "meat market" (205) in which women endure cosmetic surgery, risk starvation, and go to other desperate lengths to increase their sexual marketability. Child and spouse abuse, abandonment, poverty, male indifference and callousness, rampant pornography ("Pornomarts") and curbside prostitution ("Porneycorners," "Bun-Dle Buggies," "Feels on Wheels"), contempt for motherhood: all diminish drastically the reality of female freedom in the time before. On all points of the political compass, people begin to feel the need for a cleanup, a return to family values, a longing for safety. "Freedom from" (from violence, chaos, decadence, ennui) starts to look a lot more attractive than the previously vaunted "Freedom to" (24), and the tolerance for restrictions on civil liberties increases. Sound familiar?

Among dozens of details of the time before that will ring a bell with the reader, computerization leaps out as a necessary preparation for the Gilead coup. Compubite, Compudoc, Compucount, Compubank, Computalk, Compucard, Compunumber: all of these technological "advances" facilitate depersonalization as well as economic and political control. Atwood, writing in the mid 1980s, envisions a society where cash — anonymous, portable, powerful — has virtually disappeared; even in Offred's childhood, the only transaction for which cash was still used was the purchase of food, and Offred's remark that even that ceased later is certainly coming to pass in supermarkets of the 1990s.

Small changes, not drastic ones, mark the time before Gilead as worse off than our own time. As Offred points out, "Nothing changes instantaneously: in a gradually heating bathtub you'd be boiled to death before you knew it" (53). Atwood, in choosing the near future for the Gilead coup, avoids the science fiction problem of creating worlds too remote to force their relevance on us, realms so distant as to permit escapism rather than social insight.

How far away *is* Atwood's near future? Oddly, critics have placed Offred's narrative anywhere from the mid 1980s to the late twenty-second century. Shrewder calculators have favoured some point between 2000 and 2020 AD, working with various clues embedded in the text. I confess to an inside track on this, as I've seen Atwood's manuscript notation of Offred's birth year — 1978 — which, Offred being thirty-three during her tale-telling, would place the Handmaid in the year 2011 and the coup roughly after 2005. Atwood hesitated over that specificity, deleting and reinstating and then crossing out the birth date a second time, wisely deciding to leave the dating indeterminate. (She did, however, refer in a 1986 interview to the narrative as taking place "twenty years from now" [Hancock 216].) Nailing the narrative to a single year shortens a dystopia's shelf life, to a degree, by narrowing the applicability of the tale to a single moment (as happened at least superficially to George Orwell's *Nineteen Eighty-Four*). What matters fictively is that Atwood positioned the regime only slightly ahead of our era, so that it remains recognizably relevant; doing so gave her the latitude to extrapolate believably from the already alarming present to more extreme future events (e.g., R-strain syphilis, the classified Spheres of Influence Accord) and so make credible the dystopia she has presented.

Offred views Gilead from the angle of one cog in the new machine, one of the women who are going to save the shrinking population through their "viable ovaries." A Handmaid, after proper reeducation about her duties in the new order, is assigned to a childless couple of the elite in the hope of creating a healthy baby. In a grotesque and deliberately anti-erotic ceremony supposedly meant to replicate the biblical tale of patriarch Jacob siring a child with his wife's maidservant, the Commander copulates with "the lower half of" the Handmaid, as she lies between the legs of his Wife. If a successful pregnancy results, the birth is similarly staged (this time *with* some genuine biblical precedent), on a two-tiered birthing stool with the Wife again positioned as a sort of armchair between whose legs the Handmaid delivers. After a period of breastfeeding, the Handmaid is assigned to a new Commander, leaving her infant in the care of the previous household and feeling "comforted" by the reward that she will never be sent to the Colonies. If, however, there is no pregnancy (the unacknowledged norm since most of the Commanders, like most of the masses, are sterile), and if she fails again (it is always her fault; Gilead does not recognize the possibility of male barrenness) at two subsequent two-year postings, it's Jezebel's or the Colonies for her. Offred is on her third and final posting.

This summary is not handed to us at the beginning of the novel but revealed in "gasps" (29), the same way that Offred must glimpse the world from within her winged headgear and shrunken circumstances, the same way the average citizens of Gilead have had to sort out what is happening in their land. Offred was not, in the time before, a terribly observant person, but now she notices everything, every tiny detail, in a life where virtually all other distractions are forbidden. As she attempts to reconstruct events, take stock of her situation, reconcile past with present, and attempt strategies for survival such as tale-telling, we are drawn into those processes. We start in an unexplained gymnasium-turned-dormitory, greeted by lots of archaically costumed women but few explanations. Dependent on Offred and our own wits, we look around, begin to piece things together, deduce connections, sort through the options, do some reconstructions of our own. Some items in this odd detective story we uncover in the first few chapters, such as how Offred came to this house; others, including the Ceremony at the centre of this bizarre society, will have to wait until chapter 16; and only in chapter 28 will we finally hear details of how the Sons of Jacob managed their coup of the United States. When Professor Pieixoto at the end of his lecture on Gilead and Offred concludes with the ritual and largely rhetorical "Are there any questions?" (293), the answer will be a resounding yes.

Yet, in the course of forty-six chapters, Offred's story supplies remarkable insights and details regarding where she is coming from (literally and in the old idiom) and where she has landed. However much the professor in the "Historical Notes" may complain that she lacks "the instincts of a reporter or a spy" (292), through Offred we learn much about the mechanics, nuances, and inconsistencies of her society, as well as the connections between Gilead and the time before. And we are taken on our tour by a guide with a sense of humour and fascinating turns of mind. Standing back and studying the relationships in the novel, we see how Offred's complex connection with the Commander and his Wife over approximately five months is counterpointed by her past triangle with her husband and her mother, and how each set of relationships is haunted by a ghost baby — her confiscated daughter and her child as yet unconceived.

"SORORIZE"

Interestingly, the longest relationship in the narrative is not spousal or maternal but sisterly, in contradiction of Offred's scepticism about feminism's pronouncements on sisterhood. The one character active in all three time phases of Offred's tale is Moira, whom most readers (Offred included) regard as a sort of heroine of the novel, although obviously not the leading character or protagonist. College confidante in the time before, classmate in the Red Centre, booster of Offred's morale, and source of a lot of her (and our) information during her night out with Fred at Jezebel's, Moira is also a recurrent voice in Offred's head, urging defiance, arguing the resistive powers of parody, countering Offred's tendency to wimpishness. Moira,

Ofglen, and Mom-in-memory are a tenacious trio pressing Offred not to adapt to the unacceptable.

Atwood does not soft-pedal the price of protest, however. All three will end up dead or doomed. And Offred, who had always felt uncomfortable with such selfless radicalism, has at least one moment of snidely blaming the feminists of the time before for disastrously rocking the boat: "Mother, I think. Wherever you may be. . . . You wanted a women's culture. Well, now there is one. It isn't what you meant, but it exists. Be thankful for small mercies" (120). With that rather unkind rebuke, Offred confirms her place in the great mainstream of timid citizenry, her partial role as Everywoman. And the irony is two-edged: as a child Offred wished for more ceremony in her life; now she has it. It isn't what she meant, but it exists. Atwood neatly demonstrates the contrariness of human reactions and also rewrites the wry folk saying, "Beware what you wish for — you may get it." More important, the author heads off any potential charge that Offred was one of those uppity, educated women who brought the sexist backlash of Gilead upon themselves.

Tapping an ancient oral tradition of telling a story within a story, Atwood doubles it in twice-telling the tale of Moira's escape attempt. First we hear Offred's rendering of Aunt Lydia's version, as passed through Janine to Dolores to Alma to Offred (chapter 22). Much later (chapter 38), we hear Offred's reconstruction of Moira's own account of her break for freedom. In both narratives Offred takes responsibility for having fleshed out the story, but there are no important discrepancies between the versions. Naturally, Moira's tale significantly advances the amount of information about the regime, the resistance movement, and her fate up to and including her banishment to Jezebel's. What is most interesting to notice, however, is Offred's reactions to the two versions.

In the first case, still at the Red Centre, she and the other Handmaids savour the glimpse of audacity and liberty that their sister has provided. But Offred admits regretfully that they also find it "frightening. Moira was like an elevator with open sides. She made us dizzy. Already we were losing the taste for freedom, already we were finding these walls secure" (125). In the second version, the scene is a gauge of how much Offred has come to depend on Moira as her rebel alter ego. Hearing resignation in Moira's voice, Offred realizes how desperately she wants to believe that courage can persist and resistance can thrive against the forces of darkness. "I don't want her to be like me. Give in, go along, save her skin. . . . I want gallantry from her, swashbuckling, heroism, single-handed combat. Something I lack" (234). But a new dimension has emerged: the concerns with physical freedom/safety in the first instance now take a back seat to anxieties about artistic goals. Offred has been telling her story long enough that she has become acutely conscious of the difficulties, responsibilities, and powers of words. She frets over the inopportune circumstances under which Moira told her the tale — a lack of pen and paper, the interruptions, the necessity of haste — and reveals her highest priority: "I've tried to make it sound as much like her as I can. It's a way of keeping her alive" (228). Sex, whatever Gilead may think, is not the only way to give life.

When Professor Pieixoto accuses Offred of malice toward Serena Joy, he is flattening a very complicated relationship into a cliché of female rivalry. Agreed, there are times when Offred declares her contempt for the old woman (143, 151, 194, 247) or detects Serena's loathing of her (13, 16, 86, 90, 269, 276). And Offred is too human not to enjoy mean moments of superiority, usually related to Serena's age and barrenness or the Commander's preference for the Handmaid's company (77, 144, 151). On the other side of the ledger, however, are impulses of remarkable empathy, as when Offred, suffering from "amputated speech" (189), recognizes that Serena is mourning her own "amputated glory" (51) as a celebrity. Having mocked Serena's knitting of unwanted scarves with designs of "stiff humanoid figures" (13) as "her form of procreation" (144), she later comprehends those "geometric boys and girls in a different light: evidence of her stubbornness, and not altogether despicable" (191). Although she may harbour some resentment that the mother figure that she wants Serena to be does not save her, as something of a daughter figure (109), from what then amounts to incest, after the first Ceremony Offred is still generous enough to wonder whether the whole ordeal is worse for "her or me" (90). And in one poignant parallel scene, as she takes her plain meal in misery upstairs in her stark little room, she is sensitive to Serena's equal misery downstairs in the luxurious dining room. "I wonder how she manages to get herself noticed," Offred muses. "I think it must be hard" (62). The two women become downright conspiratorial in the plan to mate Offred with Nick, and in slipping down the stairs with Serena for the first tryst, Offred acknowledges their sisterhood under the oppressive regime: "I see the two of us, a blue shape, a red shape, in the brief glass eye of the mirror as we descend. Myself, my obverse" (243).

Similar nuances and fluctuations, although less developed, may be discerned in studying Offred's interactions with Rita and Cora. Offred takes heart in knowing there is a network of information among the Marthas, and at the end is especially regretful that she has disappointed Cora's dreams of a child. While it is accurate to see Gilead as a society in which women are deliberately divided against each other for purposes of control, and it is true that Aunt Lydia's talk about female camaraderie falls flat, there are nonetheless occasions in which a sister sense survives. The irony is that it is really not very different from paradoxes of sisterhood in the time before, when for all her closeness with her like-minded women friends, Offred's mother endured a terrible isolation and lack of support in her decision to have a child, while a bonding of such different political animals as Offred and Moira was a profound success. The call to "sororize" (11), although always a challenge outside the patriarchal language at hand, and quite beyond detection by Mr. Pieixoto, continues to be heard even in Gilead.

In my remarks on the critical reception of the text, I mentioned that readers and reviewers have tended to take strong stands on Offred as heroine or weakling. There has been a palpable feminist desire to set Offred up as a political symbol: of woman victimized, of woman resistive, of woman triumphant. In another camp, lovers of action have berated her for her passivity and her infuriating inclination to forgive her oppressors, as have those feminists who feel she lets the side down by sleeping with the enemy, as it were. Moralists lament her unworthy actions, flabby vacillations, and rationalizations. Nonmaterialists celebrate the survival of her narrative as a total success story of one woman's unflinching march to creative selfhood. All of these reactions seem to miss (or reject) the point that Atwood was creating a rounded character, not an Amazon or a position paper. However much we might delight to focus on the strong, inspiring Moira ("good choice," Offred would say), it is the ordinary, average, messily contradictory, and mostly unheroic person whose reactions to crisis intrigue Atwood. It is people like us.

Nevertheless, I was curious to see how Offred would "score" in resisting or capitulating to the new order. Her types of resistance are many: memory, fantasy, sexuality, small broken rules (match and cigarette, talks with Ofglen and Moira), large violations (Scrabble and Jezebel's with the Commander, sex with Nick), mental insolences, the hoarding of her former name, keeping a low profile, sense of humour, private pep talks, silent prayers (*Nolite te bastardes carborundorum*), and of course her narrative. However, her capitulations are also many: abuses of Janine, identification with Fred's household, rapidly decreasing taste for freedom, defense of Fred and intermittent fondness for him, complicity in Salvagings, dependence on Moira to be the rebel spirit for them both, failure to help Mayday, and the final agonized realization that to stay alive and out of physical pain she would betray "anyone. It's true, the first scream, whimper even, and I'll turn to jelly, I'll confess to any crime . . ." (267).

Two things became clear as I attempted to keep score. One was that many of the points I tallied on one side were equally valid on the other. Would suicide be resistance or surrender? How about the elementary technique of surviving tyranny: keeping one's head down and outliving it? How should one regard the wild trysts with Nick, given that both lovers are also obeying orders from Serena Joy? That's a particularly tricky one: if you see sex with Nick as giving in, then Offred's guilt and regret are resistances; if you see the affair as resistance, then her remorse and renunciation are capitulations. And compassion for Serena Joy and the Commander: is that more wimpishness, as Offred thinks, or the charity that could save the world, or both? From these conundrums sprang the second insight: that Atwood is determined to break our desire to emerge with a tidy verdict of innocent or guilty, to show that Offred, like every other character in the novel, like us, may be both simultaneously.

To me, the most neglected passage of *The Handmaid's Tale* is the moment that Offred finally understands the "true power" of totalitarianism (268). Ofglen #1 has killed herself to protect her Mayday comrades, and Offred is so scared that she abjures all relationships and all forms of resistance. She negotiates directly with the Gilead God: "I'll stop complaining. I'll accept my lot. I'll sacrifice. . . . I'll renounce." The thought flickers through her head that "this can't be right but I think it anyway." The collapse is complete: "I resign my body freely, to the uses of others. They can do what they like with me. I am abject" (268). Up to this point, the novel may be seen primarily as Gothic romance, fictive autobiography, or quest for female self-actualization, but in a gulp it becomes utterly political, a futurist projection of the dehumanizing exercise of power of which our species has always shown itself capable. It is unlike Winston's total surrender to Big Brother in *Nineteen Eighty-Four*, however, in that Offred is led away with a scrap of faith in Nick, and a glimmer of hope, and an unexpected degree of charity in her heart.

OFLUKE, OFFRED, OFNICK

Luke, Fred, Nick: Offred's male partners line themselves up in curt monosyllables, with a similar brevity of character development that makes them kin with the men in most of Atwood's fiction. Imperfectly perceived by female protagonists, riddles never solved, Atwood's fictional males seem threats one minute, saviours the next, eternal replayings of the life-giver/destroyer paradox embodied in father figures. The argument that they play something of that role in Offred's life is reinforced by the fact that she has never really had a father beyond her mother's cavalier stories of a nice fellow with blue eyes who wandered away.

Luke is a ghost presence, a necessary ingredient in the first part of Offred's tale should we take it as a romance. He is her lost love. In mulling over their courtship, marriage, parenting, and escape attempt, Offred sketches a man of solidity, competence, gentle caring, and good humour, a man who does his share of the domestic duties without a fuss and can be depended upon for support. She wants to be faithful to him, but finds the memory of him gradually fading. To fight that trend and keep him alive imaginatively, she calls upon her narrative sorcery and creates three versions of what has happened to him: a swift and merciful death; an agonized imprisonment; an escape into exile. She defends the dream of a message from him and, more audaciously, the contradiction of believing in all three scenarios simultaneously (a small triumph against the either/or thinking of Gilead, one might claim). "Whatever the truth is, I will be ready for it," she ventures tentatively (100).

Although Offred longs specifically for Luke, each time the wish modulates into a generic and self-focused desire for any warm and comforting body. And when she thinks of his protective and somewhat paternalistic reaction to the Gilead coup ("You know I'll always take care of you" [168]), four years later she still cannot decide whether her suspicion that he actually rather liked the male shift of power is or is not "Unworthy, unjust, untrue" (171). It is interesting how she elides Luke's adulterous betrayal of his first wife, and even fails to recognize as a manifestation of her own sense of guilt a dream she had about donning that wife's clothes and finding that none of them fit (70). But the involvement with Nick will cause her to feel enormous guilt, as she is pulled in two directions by the romantic ideal of fidelity and the demands of flesh and heart (not to mention, at the start, the simple temptation of an antidote to pain and boredom). After the tryst in Nick's apartment, it is psychologically and emotionally time for Luke to recede almost entirely, edited out of the personal stories she showers upon her new lover and supplanted in her daytime fantasies and nighttime retreats by reveries and realities of Nick.

When Offred takes Nick as her lean, dark, mysterious lover, she fabricates another tripartite structure, this time to describe their first sexual encounter. The first is passionate; the next is stylized, cinematic, a script from a Bogart movie; the third is sparse, distracted, guilt-ridden. She then segues into a chapter saturated with apologies for her behaviour, for her reckless obsession with Nick, for her faithlessness to Luke, for her adaptation to Gilead and surrender of the goal of freedom. She weaves romantic fantasies, takes absurd chances, pours out her secrets to a man who is laconic, unresponsive (except sexually), and of course bedding her under orders from Serena Joy. While she realizes all of that, it does not dampen her ardour, and she even goes so far as to repudiate her spirit ally, the previous Offred, on the jealous theory that Nick might once have serviced her too (254). Love is not altogether blind, however, and she recognizes that she loves an idea more than a man. "I make of him an idol, a cardboard cutout" (254). In the moment of truth, as the Van comes to get her, Offred does not hesitate to "give up Nick" (268). She also immediately assumes that he has betrayed her, and only his triple invocation — "It's Mayday," the saying of her real name, and "Trust me" (275) — allays her fears. The "Historical Notes" fall heavily on the side of regarding Nick as Mayday rescuer, but maintain ambiguity on his motives, and in their own way compound the duality of the rescuer/betrayer male figure in Gothic romance.

Sandwiched between the two younger men is the Commander,

whose style with Offred is indulgent, patronizing, "positively daddyish" (172). His substantial power in the Gilead hierarchy, verified by Ofglen, is not a prominent element in his clandestine meetings with Offred, whom he enjoys treating gallantly, doling out treats and small freedoms. In the Gothic romance tradition, he is a man of many "benevolent" guises, in one scene resembling variously a museum guard, a bank president, a vodka advertisement sophisticate, a fairy-tale shoemaker, and a father reading a bedtime story (82, 83). But never a monster. Rather, he joins Offred's long-departed father and a sizeable number of Atwood's male characters in appearing "permanently absent-minded, like they can't quite remember who they are" (115). In spite of his immense powers, he more than once gives "evidence of being truly ignorant of the real conditions under which [Handmaids live]" (149). And he surprises us by conceding that, in the improved new order, "Better . . . always means worse, for some" (198). His unexpectedly humble question to Offred, "What did we overlook?" (206), is an admission that Gilead is not really working, as is (despite his dismissal of her answer, "Love") his earlier request for a kiss "As if you meant it" (132).

That Atwood wanted not to demonize him, wanted rather to show the human, ordinary face of oppression, is evident in the draft versions of the novel, where negative and repulsive attributes were diluted and often converted into assets. For example, "his thinning hair" (box 72) became "his straight neatly brushed silver hair" (82); stale and dank smells were deleted. His "probably greenish white, tufted and pleated raw body" was trimmed down to his "white, tufted raw body" (89) and his "reddish face" turned into "his not-unpleasant face" topped by that "silver hair" (89). In the novel he is another Atwoodian male enigma, a contradiction, a man of enormous power yet disarming personality. The Latin primer he shows Offred is a perfect metaphor for this: a schoolboy mock conjugation he finds hilarious ("*pistis pants*") is scrawled obliviously on a famous picture of the rape of the Sabine women by Roman soldiers (175), and the *Nolite te* inscription that represents the last brave message of Offred's doomed predecessor is scribbled on the page opposite a defaced Venus de Milo. Although Offred harbours no illusions about her precarious status as the Commander's "whim" (149), she cannot resist the impulse to humanize him, to see him whole. At its best it is a valiant and generous rejoinder to a society determined to see its women only in parts, dismembered, Handmaid wombs or Martha hands; at its worst it is flabby, complicitous, potentially fatal sentimentality, a manifestation of female conditioning to be nice and make everything pleasant, the impulse that will "add in" boyish freckles, cowlicks (175), and firelight (172). Offred grudgingly defines herself as Fred's mistress, and uncoincidentally is suddenly reminded of an old TV interview with a Nazi commandant's mistress, who denied her man had been a monster, who had found him "endearing" (137). In that palimpsest of two mistresses' experiences, Offred realizes "How easy it is to invent a humanity, for anyone at all. . . . to make it better" (137–38). The TV story ends with the final price of collaboration, however: the German mistress's suicide.

Commander Fred clearly never operates at the same sexual level for Offred as do Luke and Nick, except in the voluptuous medium of words: Scrabble, magazines, books, dictionaries. This difference is accentuated by a conflation in which Fred takes Offred to exactly the same hotel room that she and Luke used for sex before their marriage. The contrast is dramatic: where once she felt she would die if there were to be no more sex with Luke, with Fred she is unable to "bestir" her inert body and cannot fake enthusiasm even for survival's sake. Offred makes plain that, for her, Fred's appeal lies in the body of language rather than of flesh: "The fact is that I don't want to be alone with him, not on a bed. I'd rather have Serena there too. I'd rather play Scrabble" (238). The unexpected mention of Serena underscores another echo, now actualized: where once she dreamt guiltily of wearing Luke's first wife's clothes, the metaphor has now become tangible, in the form of Serena Joy's blue cape. Offred's instinctive aversion is compounded by the implicit taboo of incest, for Fred's elderly fatherliness and Serena Joy's lingering potential as the "motherly figure, someone who would understand and protect me" (15), doubly cast Offred's relationship with the Commander as quasi-incestuous.

In the end the Commander has no power to save Offred, certainly from the Eyes, even from the wrath of his Wife, and he probably will lack sufficient power to save himself. His silver hair now looks simply "grey. He looks worried and helpless. . . . he is shrinking. There have already been purges among them, there will be more" (276). Summoning those subtle victim's counterpowers to forgive, sympathize, care, Offred stands "above him, looking down," and realizes, "I still have it in me to feel sorry for him." Her own reaction? "Moira is right, I am a wimp" (276). The reader may both agree and disagree, confirming, as Offred demonstrates with her three beliefs about Luke, the human capacity to believe opposites simultaneously.

HISTORICAL NOTES

"And so I step up, into the darkness within; or else the light" (277). These are Offred's final words to us, and after forty-six chapters of intimacy with her, it is startling and disconcerting to enter next upon what seems to be a dry and scholarly epilogue, "Historical Notes on *The Handmaid's Tale.*" "Being a partial transcript of the proceedings of the Twelfth Symposium on Gileadean Studies, held ... on June 25, 2195." Many careless reviewers have passed over it altogether as not worth mentioning, or have given it only glancing attention as an appended source of information (that perhaps Atwood hadn't been clever enough to find room for in the tale proper) or have even suggested that it is a weak attempt at satire that the reader would be well advised to skip. Only 35 of the 210 book reviews I have read gave it any comment of any sort at all, more often than not simply an allusion to it as an academic endnote or at most a timely spoof to lighten the ending of a dark tale.

Atwood has consistently downplayed any satiric intent, referring to the epilogue as an informational exercise and a signal for optimism that Gileads never last forever. Dismissing Beryl Langer's suggestion that the epilogue is "a fairly devastating comment on the academic enterprise, and the way it defuses the impact of accounts of human suffering," Atwood defended Pieixoto's approach as "just human nature! You cannot be present in the life experience of someone who lived 250 years ago the way that person is. You can try a bit harder than my academic did, but it is a very hard thing to do" ("Interview" 135). In actuality, however, this is Atwood the trickster leaving it to the alert reader to see that she is up to more than she admits; the "Historical Notes" are a crucial and complex part of Atwood's fictional strategy, containing some of the most chilling passages of an already grim novel.

It is nearly two hundred years after Offred's narrative, and the academic world — banned in Gilead, with one of its most prestigious venues (Harvard) turned into a spy centre — has had the last laugh. Not only is academe once again in business (universities, faculty, research, symposia, learned societies, international conferences, etc.) but it has reduced Gilead to a subject on the conference circuit, an object on the dissecting slabs of history departments. After the racism of Gilead, it is reassuring to see that native peoples have assumed their full place in society, as evidenced by the native names of the chair, Maryann Crescent Moon, and the conference meteorologist, Professor Johnny Running Dog. The location of the conference adds to that assumption, for the Denay (Dene) are native people of Canada's northwest, and Nunavit (Nunavut) is a huge eastern segment of the Canadian Northwest Territories slated to acquire Inuit self-government in 1999. It is a satisfying turning of the tables to have a native person, Crescent Moon, as head of a Department of Caucasian Anthropology. And after Offred's painful account of female suppression, it is a pleasure to note that the chair of this conference is female. Things seem not only "back to normal" (if we can still use that phrase unself-consciously after reading this novel), but somewhat improved.

As the chair makes her announcements and begins her introduction of the guest speaker, it seems we are in for no more than a mischievous send-up of academe. But there has already been the small colonial in-joke, more significant to Canadian than American readers, that the place of honour and cultural authority at the conference, the keynote voice, is still being accorded to Mother Britain, in the form of Professor Pieixoto from Cambridge University, England (the *real* Cambridge). In case we miss that detail, Pieixoto drives it home in derisively referring to Offred as "an educated woman, insofar as a graduate of any North American college of the time may be said to have been educated" (287). And there has been that superficially amusing mention of a Costume-Period Sing-Song, which becomes disturbing upon reflection: will everyone turn up in red habits or Econowife striped dresses or Eyes uniforms? As Ken Norris has pointed out, "It is difficult to imagine a merry band of future historians dressing up for a Third Reich Period-Costume sing-song, but Atwood's 'historical notes' suggest that just such an event may be possible at some future date" (361). The declared topic of the keynote address, an inquiry into the authenticity of Offred's story, implies that this scholar is unaware of or plans to ignore the coded warning of the conference setting, Deny None of It.

The distinguished professor begins his address very badly indeed, with a sexist joke, at the female chair's expense, which puns on the words "enjoyed" and "Chair"/"Char" (282), drawing a double parallel among food consumed, Crescent Moon, and sex with a woman; the joke is received, however, with laughter. Although he then refers with seeming modesty to "my little chat," the effect accumulates that he values his commentary well above its subject, Offred's tale. His second inappropriate joke reinforces that impression, using the title that he and his colleague have given Offred's story as the occasion not only for paying homage to Chaucer ("Predictable Eurocentric sexist choice," some would sniff unkindly) but also for deliberately (as he admits) getting in a crude little witticism on the "archaic vulgar signification of the word *tail*; that being, to some extent, the bone, as it were, of contention . . ." (283). This leering double sexual pun (tail and bone) is greeted not only with laughter but with applause. Then he outdoes himself with a joke that takes the "Underground Femaleroad," that courageous rescue network the name of which pays tribute to the pre-1861 American Underground Railroad for fleeing slaves, and conflates it mockingly into the "Underground Frailroad" (283). It would be nice to think that this third belittlement of women provokes some groans among the laughs because its humour is regarded as offensive, but chances are that what little negative response there is occurs simply because the wordplay is a clunker. One may claim that the audience laughter is just politeness or deference, but there is no question that sexism is alive and well in 2195. For a readership newly arrived from detailed exposure in Offred's tale to a society where all these small joking reductions of women were finally taken to their extreme, however, the jests are a lot less funny. In that light, it is easy to understand the annoyance of some commentators with Professor Pieixoto for his slightly pedantic reluctance (not shared by Maryann Crescent Moon) to call the transcription a "manuscript" or even "document" (282, 283), seeing him as unwilling to take female narratives and values seriously even when he's the white knight rescuing the maiden and her tale.

Pieixoto's stock may rise again with the reader as he describes his and his colleague's meticulous efforts to transcribe the tale from the thirty unnumbered tape cassettes found buried in what used to be Bangor, Maine. His paper offers useful information on Gilead, including its biblical and historical precedents and social theory, and the pre-Gilead period. We learn, realize, or are reminded of a variety of interesting matters. For example, in the time before (our time), there were precedents for providing "birth services": artificial insemination, fertility clinics, and surrogate motherhood; Gilead banned birth technology but seized upon surrogate motherhood, thus replacing "the serial polygamy common in the pre-Gilead period with the older form of simultaneous polygamy practised both in early Old Testament times and in the former State of Utah in the nineteenth century" (287). Pieixoto informs us that the sources for Gilead's practices and characteristics were highly eclectic, from the Philippines (for Salvagings) to Canada (for the colour of Handmaid outfits from Canadian World War II prisoner-of-war garb) to household products (to give the Aunts reassuringly familiar names out of the Handmaids' cosmetics and home remedies memory bank). We learn that Gilead's racist policies "were firmly rooted in the pre-Gilead period, and racist fears provided some of the emotional fuel that allowed the Gilead takeover to succeed as well as it did" (287); that there were Save the Women societies in the British Isles (again an echo of the American slavery years), and that Offred might have been able to take refuge there; — that "the Canada of that time" (292) was the end of the Underground Femaleroad, as it had been for United Empire Loyalists in the eighteenth century, black slaves in the nineteenth century, and then Vietnam war protesters in the twentieth century; that, as in the previous epochs, Canada was afraid to "antagonize" the powerful nation to her south, and therefore allowed roundups of refugees; and that Gilead, like all totalitarian regimes, had a tendency to eat its own in purge after purge. Since "the Gileadean regime was in the habit of wiping its own computers and destroying printouts after various purges and internal upheavals" (285), it becomes apparent that the surviving records of Gilead are less complete than Offred's. In other words, in this case at least, woman words have had more staying power, her-story has outlived his-story, and Offred has far more of the last word than Fred does. Further, Offred's accounts of the circumstances of the Sons of Jacob coup and of the pre-Gilead conditions are no less detailed and arguably much more so than the professor's, for all he may think her uninformed.

From Pieixoto's tidy analysis and detached overview, several points stand out in shocking relief. One is that Offred "was among the first wave of women recruited for reproductive purposes" (286). If we had hoped from the ambiguous ending to the tale that the Mayday underground was gaining control and the end of the regime was in sight, no such luck! We were merely at the beginning of Early Gilead, to be followed inexorably by the increasingly severe Middle and Late Gilead.

A second shock is that, as Atwood has reiterated in various interviews, everything in Gilead has happened before, somewhere, sometime. Pieixoto explains the political science truism: "As we know from the study of history, no new system can impose itself upon a previous one without incorporating many of the elements to be found in the latter ... and Gilead was no exception to this rule" (287). To put it another way, everything is based to a degree on that which preceded it, no matter how different it appears. Gilead's roots are in the time before, and the time before is our own time. However bizarre we may think Gilead, its core ideas are nothing new, and all of its practices are already on the human record. We move closer to a chilling understanding of Aunt Lydia's observation: "The Republic of Gilead ... knows no bounds. Gilead is within you" (23).

A third truly striking remark in Pieixoto's presentation has to do with a major technique of oppression familiar to social scientists, wherein the best way to control a group is to use members of that group as controllers. In Gilead, then, the "most cost-effective way to control women for reproductive and other purposes was through women themselves" (290). Hence the Aunts. Small perks, personal security, and the pleasures of power seal the deal. It's a classic depiction of Victim Position #1, as described in Atwood's analysis of victimhood in her literary study *Survival*.

One of Pieixoto's statements in the middle of his address would probably go down smoothly if delivered without a context, but in its placement after our Handmaid's tale, it is deeply objectionable. He warns, not unreasonably (but definitely out of character), against the vanities of "hypocritical self-congratulation" (284) in the study of earlier periods, what might be called the aren't-they-dumb-aren't-we-so-much-smarter mindset. But then Pieixoto concludes, to applause, ". . . we must be cautious about passing moral judgement upon the Gileadeans. Surely we have learned by now that such judgements are of necessity culture-specific. . . . Our job is not to censure but to understand" (284). As a generality, this may seem acceptable, but we have witnessed too much of the brutalities of Gilead to be willing to forgo our moral standards this soon. Pieixoto's objection to any "culture-specific" condemnation can be subjected to a litmus test: let us substitute the Holocaust (or whatever event we regard as indisputably evil) for Gilead and see if it still seems appropriate to reject moral judgement.

For many readers this is the particular point, if not before, at which Pieixoto's scholarly authority starts to dissolve. It is hard to rely on his ability to pronounce upon the "authenticity" of Offred's narrative when it appears that he understands it so little as to think she has provided us with only "crumbs" of information about Gilead (292). It is difficult also to trust his values when we hear him lament Offred's inadequacies and pine for "even twenty pages or so of print-out from Waterford's [Commander Fred's] private computer" (292), knowing that in a heartbeat he would trade the entirety of this woman's extraordinary living account for a few of that man's executive files. As Ken Norris puts it neatly, to Professor Pieixoto "history is Hitler's working papers, not Anne Frank's diary" (363). There is no doubt that he privileges official history (his-story) over the traditionally dismissed alternate historical accounts of domestic diary, private correspondence, and female autobiography (her-story).

Admitting twice that much of his exposition is "guesswork" (284, 292) and conceding that historians "cannot always decipher [the voices of history] precisely in the clearer light of our own day" (293), Pieixoto nonetheless is confident that "further research" (284) of the type he favours can illuminate most of the "great darkness" of history (293). Worried about forgeries and hoaxes, he appears to be a traditionalist who still believes in a sharp line between history (true) and fiction (invented, not true). Certainly, despite his academic pedigree he little understands how thoroughly Offred's subtle narrative undermines the proposition that historians can pin down the truth — even the most sincere commentator can never get it exactly right, can never draw an unwavering boundary between fact and fiction. It might be that, lacking her humility, he also lacks her wisdom. And it might be also that Atwood is having some sly postmodern fun with those who would reject her cautionary vision as "just" fiction.

In insisting that she is merely "one of many, and must be seen within the broad outlines of the moment in history of which she was a part" (287), Pieixoto smudges Offred's individuality. He complains that she "does not see fit to supply us with her original name" (287), indicating his disinclination or inability to follow her clues to the possible name that many astute readers have sleuthed out: June. He rests all of his faith that the tale is authentic not on the myriad, almost unfakable details of Offred's account or on the cumulative power of its telling but instead on the assurances of his recording experts "that the physical objects themselves [the tape cassettes] are genuine" (284–85).

Perhaps most strikingly, Pieixoto soon drops Offred to attend to his real interest: the male power elite of Gilead. Still believing in history as the story of the powerful, Pieixoto shows no recognition of the widely accepted stance that the personal is political, and that the stories of the marginalized matter as much and perhaps more. Analysis of the distribution of topics in Pieixoto's talk is extremely revealing on this point. Eight percent of his presentation is devoted to bad jokes and framing remarks. Thirty-nine percent is a description of his and Wade's research techniques and information about Gilead (the latter being sometimes rather elementary material to be delivering to the *twelfth* symposium on Gileadean Studies, and a lot of it repetitive of material given to us more compellingly by Offred). Thirty-one percent is speculation on the two possible identities of Commander Fred, marked by Pieixoto's admiration for the candidates' totalitarian skills. We may become increasingly uncomfortable with the speaker's diction for Gileadean tactics and tacticians — "genius" (289), "ingenuity" (290), "brilliant" (290) — and it is startling to hear him allude positively to a policy of suppression of women as being "credited" (289) to Commander Frederick Judd. Pieixoto glosses over a period of purges as merely "cautious" (292) and speculates that Nick's "wiser course" (293) might have been to assassinate rather than assist Offred. In the same vein, one of Judd's creations that Pieixoto particularly commends is the "crack female control agency known as the 'Aunts' " (290), whose pseudo-militarism and total complicity with the elite earn them five percent of the professor's lecture time. Nick, both for his (probable) power as an Eye and for his (likely) participation in the "quasi-military" Mayday underground (291), merits six percent of the professor's interest. So how much is left for Offred and her story, the putative centre of Pieixoto's concern, the focus of his scholarly research? She is given a humble eleven percent of his attention, and half of that time is consumed by his concluding roster of unanswered questions about her ultimate fate. In according little over one-tenth of his presentation to the woman and the narrative that an entire regime has tried but failed to erase from history, the professor is coming dangerously near to doing the same thing two hundred years later.

THE BODY OF THE TALE

"A lot of writing," Margaret Atwood has said, ". . . is getting the right structure" ("Q&Q Interview" 67). That she got it right from the start with *The Handmaid's Tale* is suggested both by the rapidity with which she wrote the novel and by her comparative lack of tinkering with the manuscript as it emerged from her pen. (She still does first drafts by hand.) In examining the repositionings of material in the Atwood archives (box 72), I was struck by her assured plunging into the first nineteen pages — what most writers consider a terrifying stage since major structural errors in the beginning will skew disastrously the entire unfolding of the work. Nor did I find the rest of the manuscript heavily edited and rearranged. This suggests that Atwood had a remarkably clear idea of how the narrative should unfold.

The novel has not struck all readers as tightly and effectively organized, however. Some traditionalist critics have complained that the plot line jumps about, or plods and stops and plods again, or shuttles illogically among the phases of Offred's life. They denounce as unreliable and alienating a storyteller who delivers multiple versions of a single episode, and they challenge the necessity of so many apparently pointless domestic details, rambling memories, and word games. Offred seems to some readers a bored and trapped mind wandering aimlessly in a purposeless maze. A majority of critics concede that all of those effects exist but defend them as deliberately created and far from purposeless.

Thinking about the structure of *The Handmaid's Tale* is a complicated and multilayered project because there is more than one cook stirring the pot. We have Offred, apologizing for her story being "in fragments, like a body caught in crossfire or pulled apart by force," defiantly adding, "But there is nothing I can do to change it" (251). We have Professor Pieixoto admitting in the "Historical Notes" that he and his colleague could only guess at the correct order of the tapes they then transcribed to produce the Handmaid's story, but not also conceding that two male academics might have imposed on a female narrative a gendered sense of sequence. We have the reader, "You" (38), able to carry several narratives in one brain, but perhaps alternating between confusion and admiration at the braiding of three time lines: the time before Gilead, the Red Centre memories, and Offred's time in Commander Fred's household. And of course we have author Atwood behind the scenes, presumably making all the structural choices.

If we concentrate on Atwood as crafter of it all, what strikes some as a lack of internal organization may be argued to be her deliberate device to replicate the choppiness of interrupted personal journals and oral accounts, to present a narrative that feels immediate and intuitive (usually characterized as female) rather than deliberate and linear (often thought of as male). As we read Offred's words, they seem urgent, they seem to represent what is happening now, and too visibly artful a narrative crafting would interfere with that effect of spontaneity. Another line of defense would begin from the fact that Offred's life is so boring that the slightest variation in routine is welcome, and even a scratched message in the woodwork can occupy her interest for weeks. At one point she speaks of the tedium in the context of an agricultural development. "Sometime in the eighties they invented pig balls, for pigs who were being fattened in pens. Pig balls were large coloured balls; the pigs rolled them around with their snouts. The pig marketers said this improved their muscle tone; the pigs were curious, they liked to have something to think about" (65). Offred concludes wistfully, "I wish I had a pig ball." A novelistic structure that captures that tedium, that documents the tiny mind exercises and free-associations with which the narrator keeps madness at bay, is making form fit content.

If Offred's story *is* a shot-up body caught in fictional crossfire, let us attempt to rearticulate its skeleton, to re-member the body of the novel. *The Handmaid's Tale* presents us with forty-six chapters, divided into fifteen titled sections, plus an unnumbered epilogue. The eight odd-numbered sections are all comprised of single chapters, brief (two to seven pages long), entitled "Night" (except for one mild variant: "Nap"), and focused, until the final two, upon memories of the Red Centre and the time before Gilead came into being. It is under cover of night, less visible and vulnerable to the Eyes, that Offred can indulge uninterrupted in several of her many strategies for staying sane: remembering an alternative life, consciously composing a subversive story, and reflecting on the multiple views of reality and history that defy the absolutism of Gilead and its official versions. Six of the seven alternating, even-numbered sections reinforce the diary quality of the novel by taking their titles from daytime functions and authorized sites in Gilead: "Shopping," "Waiting Room," "Household," "Birth Day," "Soul Scrolls," and "Salvaging." The one exception (comparable to the daytime "Nap" in the Night sections) is "Jezebel's," which is set at night and is hardly officially sanctioned. By far the longest section — nine chapters compared with the usual four or five — "Jezebel's" interestingly draws together in one extended section Gilead's pious public face (Prayvaganzas), its corrupt underbelly (the brothel), and the entire process of negotiation and delivery of a picture of Offred's lost daughter. Further, it completes Offred's ruminations on the Red Centre and on the time before. After that Jezebel section, the subsequent Night section "records" both poignantly and ironically the first tryst with Nick, as the action begins to gallop through the Salvaging, Particicution, and arrival of Ofglen's replacement, to climax in Offred's collapse and the denouement of her ambiguous departure. The scholarly annotations thereafter, while removed by almost two centuries from their subject, can be shown to have direct links both to Gilead and to the time before.

Within that macrostructure, with its orderly alternation of day and night, there are other organizing principles at work. One is the interweaving of three time lines within Offred's tale: the time before, indoctrination at the Rachel and Leah Re-education Centre, and Offred's stay at Commander Fred's. Memories of the Red Centre comprise the shortest strand, appearing in only nine of the forty-six chapters and disappearing just as the affair with Nick begins, when the Aunts' brainwashing ebbs to its least potent. Extensive soliloquies about the time before and Offred's lost child, husband, mother, and former life naturally are much more numerous than Red Centre passages, showing up in nineteen chapters. While they are part of her daily life as well, it is above all in the privacy of her room, usually in the darkness which protects her from the Eyes, that Offred permits herself (or is driven) to revisit her pre-Gilead life. Those often painful memories dominate all six of the "Night" and "Nap" chapters up to Offred's mating with Nick, but conspicuously vanish as soon as that happens. Expressing guilt and confusion over her emotional abandonment of her former family, Offred will confess to the reader, with shame but also with a type of romantic pride that she herself views ironically, that she no longer wishes to escape, that she wants only to be there with Nick. "I have made," she rationalizes, "a life for myself, here, of a sort" (255). The span from that point until the final "Night" and her stepping into history is a mere five short chapters, whereupon a new, fourth temporal locus takes over, the Nunavit conference of 2195.

Having started by conceding that the tale often seems a jumble and arguing that it is deliberately crafted that way for rhetorical and form-content reasons, I have by now tipped my hand that *The Handmaid's Tale* actually has a tightly organized superstructure. Now I will go a step further and claim that the same is true with the internal structure, that chapters that appear to meander (and effectively replicate Offred's rambling thoughts in so doing) are in fact more coherently constructed than they seem at first reading.

This assertion may, I believe, be illustrated by tracking the line of topics in any chapter. Testing my premise, I selected a couple of chapters — one about Offred's daily life at the Commander's (chapter 5) and one about her night sortie beyond the compound to Jezebel's (chapter 35) — to see if their internal logic could be detected. In both cases I found the continuity of thought, comment, and action quite decipherable. Allow me to demonstrate.

In chapter 5, in the "Shopping" section, Offred and Ofglen go to buy groceries, in the course of which excursion we acquire information both public (about the streets, stores, nonverbal shop signs, trade practices, politics, policing, and public deportment) and private (such as the nuanced reactions to one Handmaid's pregnancy, Offred's missing Moira, and Offred's care to protect her thoughts from detection). But within the general parameters of a shopping trip, Atwood constructs a sub-commentary about the time before Gilead, one that seamlessly includes such disparate items as Offred's footwear, Bogart movies, urban hazards, and plastic bags. The connections are traceable. For instance, walking past a store where their Handmaid dresses (called habits) are purchased, Offred converts the word "habit" to its alternate meaning of "custom," and the observation that "Habits are hard to break" (24) leads her thoughts smoothly into memories of the past. Once situated in the time before, she is geared to remember the former function of another store they pass, called Lilies, which was a movie house popular for its springtime Humphrey Bogart festivals, the female stars of which (Bacall, Hepburn) were icons of female independence, wearers of blouses with defiantly and provocatively undone buttons. In a wordplay rather like the one in chapter 22 about Moira's escape, a woman on the loose, and loose women, undone buttons bespeak undone women, women having the freedom to choose to be undone. That decadent thought triggers the memory of Aunt Lydia's counterpoint that we were a society dying of too much choice. The flow of this stream of consciousness is typical of Offred's narrative.

Let us test another chapter, 35, in the lengthy "Jezebel's" section of the novel. Offred kills time until dinner, and the only concrete action is a visit from Serena Joy with the promised photograph of Offred's confiscated daughter. Yet the narrative manages to introduce wordplay on "invalid," "falling," "working out," "waiting"; analysis of romantic love; insights into the obliterations of official history; doubts, fears, and terrors about men in the time before; and contemplations on the pre-Gilead addiction to change. Take just the first of these. Offred, awaiting her dinner tray in her room, feels like a shut-in, an "invalid" (210); an invalid is one who has been "invalidated," judged valueless, rejected; passports deemed invalid prevent a crossing of borders; "no exit" is the final extrapolation, which leads directly into agonizing memories of her and Luke's attempt to escape across the Gilead border into Canada less than four years earlier. A detailed description follows of their tortured wait at the border checkpoint before they realize their invalid papers have been detected, make a break for freedom, and . . . the memory becomes too painful to continue. Offred considers consciously her options as narrator at that point: lapse into silence, withdraw into a fatal inner world, resist (*Nolite te...*) or not, or choose something more bearable to contemplate, such as the nature of romantic love. The narrative moves coherently in this new direction.

Drawn into thinking of the events of the story as being narrated as they are happening, readers may then find it a jolt to deduce from the concluding "Historical Notes" that the tale was composed later from the safety and relative freedom of a refuge to which Offred was taken after Fred's, where she had access to a tape recorder. Certain passages that seemed in a first reading to confirm the synchronicity of the action and the narrative are suddenly ambiguous. For example, Offred says, "When I get out of here, if I'm ever able to set this down, in any form, even in the form of one voice to another, it will be a reconstruction then too, at yet another remove" (126); "out of here" abruptly shifts from out of Fred's to out of the halfway house (probably in Bangor, Maine, where the tapes were discovered), and "set this down" becomes the dream of writing, part of Offred's ongoing love affair with the written word, unsatisfied by oral snippets buried on the antique music tapes. It also shifts the emphasis more fully from her longing to escape to her much more often mentioned anxiety to tell her story as accurately as possible.

The title signals it: a tale is to be told. The narrator is fully aware of the connections between her tale and herself, her self. "I compose myself" (62), she puns on the dual meanings of "compose": gain control and create. Offred remembers the time before as living "in the blank white spaces at the edges of print. It gave us more freedom. We lived in the gaps between the stories" of mutilation and murder in the daily newspapers (53). Choosing not to be visible or heard, they avoided being (as Aunt Lydia would put it later) "penetrated" (28). Now she has been thrust into a world where, apart from "mouldy old Rachel and Leah stuff" (84), the only storytellings permitted or rewarded are informing on others or testifying against oneself. "At Testifying, [the Handmaids soon learn] it's safer to make things up than to say you have nothing to reveal" (67). Ironically, then, the Red Centre may be credited with unintentionally training Offred in a skill she needs to survive, to resist being erased by Gilead and official history.

Storytelling is a universal impulse (even the male elite at Jezebel's indulge in it), and everyone's favourite story is usually his or her own. But when the story is horrific (a lost child [71]) or the subject is brutal (Salvagings [257]) or exhausting (Birth Day [121]), Offred has difficulty continuing. Indeed, in the recounting of their failed escape attempt, she flatly calls a halt. "I don't want to be telling this story. I don't have to tell it. I don't have to tell anything, to myself or to anyone else" (211), she announces defiantly. In the next few moments, she wrestles with the temptation of suicidal withdrawal, rebukes herself for her weakness, and, leaving the escape story forever unfinished (the better to control the ending?), she shifts her mind to something bearable, her discussion with Commander Fred about the nature of love. While it has been a tense sequence, there has never been any question that she would continue her tale, no matter what forces might conspire to silence her. She and all the marginalized voices she represents are like Serena's subversive garden, full of "buried things bursting upwards, wordlessly, into the light, as if to point, to say: Whatever is silenced will clamour to be heard, though silently" (143). Resistance feeds itself on stories of the audacity of others, as the regime finally realizes when it stops preceding Salvagings with detailed accounts of the crimes of the convicted because the practice has been the stimulus for a "rash" of copycat crimes (259).

Early on Offred realizes the complexities of the relationship among story, teller, and listener, as well as the ambiguities of the boundaries between story and truth. She crams into one passage a number of simply phrased but densely packed reflections on this relationship that one could annotate endlessly. She wishes she could believe that she were telling a fiction, since that buffer against harsh reality would increase her chances of staying sane. The notion that it is a fiction that she is creating also gives her the authority to control the ending, to insist that the story will end "and real life will come after it." But that illusion is one she cannot permit herself: "It isn't a story I'm telling." Swerving in a related direction she muses on what critics might call the mode of production, the fact that she is composing her life story spontaneously "in my head, as I go along" (37). (That clause, "as I go along," allows the narrative to seem immediate and still make sense when we learn the tale is told after the fact, as she goes along in recording it.) Narration also implies a narratee, somebody listening to the story; it's a comforting thought even if it should be another illusion. She can think of her story as a letter to the future. "*Dear You*, I'll say. Just *you*, without a name. Attaching a name attaches *you* to the world of fact, which is riskier, more hazardous: who knows what the chances are out there, of survival, yours? . . . *You* can mean thousands" (37–38). Rewriting René Descartes' famous "I think, therefore I am," she will assert later, "I tell, therefore you are" (251). And as she warms to her task somewhat, she becomes increasingly concerned to get the right word. "I am leashed, it looks like, manacled; cobwebbed, that's closer" (191). When your survival depends upon it, accuracy is not an idle goal.

We have a taleteller and we have an audience — so what's the problem? It's the impossibility of meeting that goal, of telling a tale accurately. Again and again Offred scrupulously warns us that her tales are reconstructions, befuddled by faulty memory (221), by devastating emotions (80), by interruptions and haste (228). She admits understanding a narrator's power to slant a description ("His hair is grey. Silver, you might call it if you were being kind" [54]), and freely confesses to doctoring her tale, adding firelight (172) or thunder (246) or sexual banter (246). She also longs to cheat a bit and tell stories of Moira's heroic escape or resistance. "I'd like her to end with something daring and spectacular, some outrage, something that would befit her." But the fact is, "I don't know how she ended . . ." (234). With Luke and again with Nick, she goes through three versions of stories of destiny and love; some of us, brought up on TV game shows, wait for the real version to please stand up, but Offred cannot oblige us. Ironically, many critics have therefore dismissed Offred as an "unreliable" narrator, whereas my view is that I trust her all the more for her scrupulous honesty. She leaves absolutes for Commanders and Professors, arguing that

> It's impossible to say a thing exactly the way it was, because what you say can never be exact, you always have to leave something out, there are too many parts, sides, crosscurrents, nuances; too many gestures, which could mean this or that, too many shapes which can never be fully described, too many flavours, in the air or on the tongue, half-colours, too many. (126)

All of this commendable reluctance notwithstanding, Offred finds, as she moves far along in her tale, that she has developed a substantial sense of responsibility toward both subjects and audience. Apart from self-interest, she sees the telling of Moira's story as precisely as possible as a "way of keeping her alive" (228), of not letting Gilead obliterate her friend or her friend's spirit. She also feels she owes something to *you*, "After all you've been through" (252) listening to what she judges to be an embarrassingly inadequate tale, "this sad and hungry and sordid, this limping and mutilated story" (251): "you deserve whatever I have left, which is not much but includes the truth" (252), a truth in which she looks even worse than she already feels she does. What comes next is a ruthlessly unvarnished and self-condemning account of her affair with Nick, the Salvaging and Particicution, and her final days at the Commander's house. Her incentive for this moral exactitude is once again that she earns her audience, *you*, who are the confirmation that she exists.

FROM TWISTED SISTER TO TWISTED SCRIPTURE

In a novel about a theocracy, one naturally expects a lot of high-profile religious allusions. But Gilead, *The Handmaid's Tale*, and Atwood have some surprises to offer in that area. Most conspicuous is the locking up of the founding text, the Holy Bible, as an incendiary document. Going further, the Sons of Jacob clamp down on all corollary materials, such as hymns, with provocative content; "Amazing Grace" crosses the line to perdition with the word "free" (51) and finds itself in the same banned category as Elvis Presley and his "Heartbreak Hotel" (51). More predictable than the paranoia about texts is that about sects, and after only a preliminary tolerance of those who declared themselves "some sort of Christian," the "sectarian round-ups began in earnest" of Quaker and Catholic, Jehovah's Witness and Baptist (232). The philosophical contradiction of a "totalitarian theocracy" resolved itself for Gilead in the theocracy (situating authority in God) being mere window dressing for the totalitarians (situating authority in themselves).

From this derives another unexpected characteristic of Gilead: the absence of a religious apparatus. The only church we see has been converted into a museum celebrating its Puritan heritage (well, its clothes and stern demeanours, mostly), and the only other even faintly churchlike building is significantly part of the Eyes' headquarters. Further, there are no (surviving) ministers or priests, only Commanders (who don't know Scripture) and Aunts (who misquote it) to spread the Word. Soul Scrolls exist to fill the gap, but they are entirely mechanical and confined to just five official and endlessly repetitive prayers, one of which is a rather unspiritual request for wealth. The only congregations we see are highly secular affairs, witnessing to such matters of this world as arranged mass weddings, military victories, and executions.

An underground but discernible contempt for what are under-stood by almost all to be the trappings of piety is reinforced by the formulaic language that is demanded. Greeting with "Blessed be the fruit" (Luke 1.42), responding with "May the Lord open" (Gen. 29.31), filling in time with "Praise be," and bidding farewell with the ominous "Under His Eye" serve to substitute for any real and potentially subversive conversation, encourage a hollow public piousness, and remind everyone of both the procreational agenda and the realities of tight surveillance in Gilead. Even the delivery of a sanctioned clause like "As the Lord is my witness" must be properly modulated (122), not overly enthusiastic, or it may have "the force of a denial" (123). Damned if you do, damned if you don't!

That little quip leads into one of the most entertaining aspects of the Gilead "theocracy": the misapplication and misquotation, both deliberate and accidental, of biblical passages and references, creating ironic, deconstructive, and/or darkly comic effects. Some amusing examples are the paeans to the eternal male religion of automobiles: the cars named Whirlwind (Jer. 23.19, Hos. 8.7), Chariot (2 Kings 2.11), and the chunky Behemoth (Job 40.15). More ironic are the names of the shops, such as "Milk and Honey," which is a Joshua (5.6) reference to a land of great prosperity, applied to a grocery store always short on produce, long on queues, in the economically dis-rupted new republic. "Lilies of the Field" for the Handmaids' dress shop is a wry choice, for the relevant passages (Luke 12.27–28, Matt. 6.28–30) speak of the lowly flowers ("they toil not, neither do they spin") as more beautifully clothed than the great King Solomon, and promise such lovely adornment (red robe and white wings? and a work-free life-style?) for those who join the faithful. "All Flesh" for the butcher's shop is particularly sly, as the reference is to Isaiah 40.6–7, wherein we are reminded of the fate of all flesh: to wither and die. "Loaves and Fishes" (Matt. 15.32–38) and "Daily Bread" (the Lord's Prayer, Matt. 6.11) exploit a contrast between their biblical reference to plenty and the miserable foodstuffs they manage (if at all) to stock.

The biblical names in *The Handmaid's Tale* all reward similar inquiry. Gilead, Children of Ham, Rachel and Leah, "Balm in Gilead" (versus Moira's "Bomb in Gilead," 205), the Book of Job, Angels of the Apocalypse, Jezebel, the Whore of Babylon: all come out of a revered and spiritually multilayered context and all are applied manipulatively but not often with sophistication to the agenda of a regime spiritually bankrupt from the start. The effects range from funny to darkly satiric.

Offred, despite her lapses of memory about the past, has a good ear for tampering in quotations. She catches and corrects Aunt Lydia's "All flesh is weak" to "All flesh is grass" (43). She also detects truncations, as in Aunt Lydia's "You must cultivate poverty of the spirit. Blessed are the meek. She didn't go on to say anything about inheriting the earth" (60). And she knows how often they mess around with one of their favourite texts, the Beatitudes (Matt. 5.3–11). "*Blessed are the silent.* I knew they made that up, I knew it was wrong, and they left things out too, but there was no way of checking" (84). Doing some of that checking on Offred's behalf, we discover that Aunt Lydia has cut off "Blessed are the merciful" without adding a promise Gilead is unlikely to keep: "for they shall obtain mercy." And sometimes it is left for the reader to track down the deliberate misquotations, as in Aunt Lydia's "From each according to her ability; to each according to his needs." "It was from the Bible," Offred says, but adds doubtfully, "or so they said" (111). In fact, it's from Karl Marx, and should read "according to his" on both sides of the semicolon. Monkeyed with, it is turned into a mandate for female servitude and male exploitation. Milton fares only marginally better: "They also serve who only stand and wait," he concluded in his sonnet on blindness, "When I Consider How My Light Is Spent." Aunt Lydia, thinking it is from the Bible, has her blindered "girls" memorize the line (18, 49) to accept the necessity of their passivity in Gilead, a society that shreds poets and the physically imperfect, but makes an art form of moral and social blindness.

More disconcerting is the use of biblical texts as justification for outrages and atrocities. The obvious case is Genesis 30.1–18 regarding Rachel and her handmaid, which Commander Fred reads before each Ceremony. Fred carries on beyond the three verses of the first epigraph, reminding us that Leah and Rachel were sisters locked in a competition, both using their handmaids in the race to come up with the most babies for their mutual husband Jacob. Although the Bible presents it blandly as the origin of the twelve tribes of Israel, to today's reader that hardly seems a worthy incident on which to base population planning. The resettlement of the Children of Ham,

64

described by "the reassuring pink face" on the TV screen (79) as proceeding on schedule, cloaks in a reference to one of Noah's sons the racist banishment of all people of colour to reservations euphemistically called National Homelands. In the same vein, Gilead's anti-Semitism is buried in a reference to Jewish people as the original Sons of Jacob, deserving of repatriation to Israel; through the "Historical Notes" we learn that this exiling from Gilead was to become wholesale slaughter when privatization of the emigration process resulted in the dumping of Jews in mid Atlantic to "maximize profits" (289). Gilead depends heavily on texts from St. Paul and from pre-Christian testaments to justify their misogyny and their violent social practices. The Scriptures read at the mass wedding (1 Tim. 2.9–15), at the Particicution (Deut. 22.23–29), at the Red Centre regarding the miseries of childbirth (Gen. 3.16), and at the monthly Ceremony (Gen. 30.1–18 and 2 Chron. 16.9) are quoted accurately, but have been lifted out of context for the darkest purposes of social control.

The route from the time before to this godless theocracy is a fairly direct one. Offred, exposed young to television's Saturday morning *Growing Souls Gospel Hour*, viewed the program only when she couldn't find cartoons. In young womanhood she quickly joined her peers in reversing "God is Love" to "Love is God": "we believed in Love, abstract and total. We were waiting, always, for the incarnation. That word, made flesh" (211). When she lists what the glossy women's magazines of the time before promised, it is an earthly equivalent of Christianity's spiritual enticements: rejuvenation, pain overcome and transcended, endless love, and immortality; modern times modified that into a secular religion of self-improvement and perpetual progress. Remembering the Bibles left by Bible Societies in hotels of the time before, Offred reflects that "probably no one read them very much" (48); in Gilead nobody but Commanders are allowed to read them, and it appears they do so only on ceremonial occasions.

In the course of her narrative Offred several times attempts personal prayer, and those moments are marked by a simple honesty in stunning contrast to the expressions of fake piety that surround her and are required of her. Watching Commander Fred read the Bible, she remarks at two levels: "He has something we don't have, he has the word. How we squandered it, once" (84). When she then is enjoined to silent prayer before the Ceremony, she uncomprehend-ingly (but actually very appropriately) tries out *Nolite te bastardes carborundorum* as a prayer: ". . . it will have to do, because I don't know what else I can say to God. Not right now" (86). Her memory takes her back to Moira's beaten feet, and her prayer concludes with an unconsciously sharper *Nolite te* and the distressed question to God: "Is this what you had in mind?" (87). Late that night, recalling her family's faces as "flickering like the images of saints, in old foreign cathedrals, in the light of the drafty candles; candles you would light to pray by . . . hoping for an answer" (97), she admits to the necessity of belief, of faith when in reduced circumstances, but repudiates some of her trench faith as "junk" (99). We are reminded of the Faith cushion in her room, and the way she wonders where its companions "Hope" and "Charity" have gone. The words "In hope" now present themselves — she cannot help but hope — but she raises some unanswerable questions about that gravestone phrase (106). One might argue that Offred in herself becomes the spokesperson for "Charity," for example in the selfless concern (what she thinks is wimpishness) she extends to Fred and Cora even as she is being led away. So faith, hope, and charity can be located, but the compromised condition of them and of her spirituality is underscored by her agonized reconstruction of the Lord's Prayer, the only verse of which to emerge unaltered and unannotated is "Deliver us from evil" (183). The God she is addressing at that point is a patient, loving, New Testament God, one with whom she sympathizes, one she does not want to disappoint. At the end of the day, however, the God she prays to, before whom she prostrates herself, is an Old Testament God, and the blessing for which she will give up all else is survival. "Dear God, I think, I will do anything you like. Now that you've let me off, I'll obliterate myself, if that's what you really want; I'll empty myself, truly, become a chalice. . . . I want to keep on living, in any form" (268).

NAME GAME

Long before Professor Pieixoto explains it, readers figure out the simple system of Handmaid naming in Gilead. Along with every-thing else, a Handmaid is stripped of her name from the time before, and thereafter called the possessive preposition "of" plus the

Christian name of the Commander to whom she is assigned: Of-fred, Of-wayne, Of-warren, Of-charles (fused to him without any arm's-length hyphen: thus, Offred). Upon completion of a posting, she will forfeit that name and assume another in a new household. We, in pre-Gilead North America, are not in a tremendously strong position to denounce this system, given as many of our society still are to the convention of a female shedding her family name and adopting that of her husband, indeed in formal situations disappearing altogether (e.g., Mrs. Fred Waterford). For us, however, it *is* theoretically voluntary.

In the opening scene of the novel, the Handmaids at the Red Centre are furtively exchanging one of their few possessions, their original names: "Alma. Janine. Dolores. Moira. June" (4). As we read the novel, we tick off the names in this list and, finding only "June" unaccounted for, may surmise that that is Offred's real name. It probably is. But Atwood chooses not to verify that deduction, I think for several very good reasons. First, Atwood has a reputation for enjoying presenting her audience with teasers and puzzles, but she is also legendary for disconcerting them with the realization that there may not be any certain answers. As well, she honours Offred's preservation of her name as a "buried" treasure (80), a comforting and protective amulet with which to resist the regime's attempt to erase her identity. The importance accorded to this one seemingly small oppression among so many huge ones also demonstrates the lengths to which the authorities are going to eradicate all direct connections between words and the identity of virtually anything (shop signs being another, less devastating casualty). And our uncertainty on this one little but important detail replicates the profound disorientation and disruption to identity that come from being deprived of so basic a descriptor as a name. This reality is brought home most tellingly in a scene that Karen Stein (271) regards as the most chilling of the novel: Offred after the Salvaging is expecting to meet Ofglen for their usual shopping trip; instead she is greeted by a stranger who now bears that name. "Ofglen, wherever she is, is no longer Ofglen. I never did know her real name. That is how you can get lost, in a sea of names" (265). The fragility of personal identity, the infinite interchangeability, and the virtual impossibility of keeping connected in Gilead are brought forcefully home in this terrible moment.

One of the namings that shows the Sons of Jacob's close attention to the details of control is that of the Aunts. Pieixoto speaks admiringly of "the notion that the Aunts should take names derived from commercial products available to women in the immediate pre-Gilead period, and thus familiar and reassuring to them — the names of cosmetic lines, cake mixes, frozen desserts, and even medicinal remedies" (290). Helena Rubenstein and Elizabeth Arden cosmetics, Lydia Pinkham's Little Pink Pills for relief of small womanly discomforts (in the nineteenth century reportedly loaded with narcotics to keep Mommy utterly mellow), and Sara Lee frozen desserts: from these products designed to "help" women look pretty, assuage their minor ailments, and save time in the kitchen were taken names for Aunt Helena, Aunt Elizabeth, Aunt Lydia, and Aunt Sara. And the group name "Aunts" was obviously intended to invoke warm memories of benevolent older female relatives, founts of sound advice and sage direction. Of course, in viewing these packaging tactics as "brilliant" psychological strategies, the professor slides over the reality that one poke with an Aunt's cattle prod would pretty well cancel whatever positive aura emanated from a fake relative whose name invoked obsolete female products.

Although the Commanders' Wives presumably are allowed to retain their names from the time before, there is no textual confirmation of that; the nearest we get is Offred's imagining a conversation among the Wives in which one is addressed as "Mildred" (109). Thus the Wives seem to be little more than their tiny roles, robbed of individual names along with their freedoms. In Fred's household, Offred is never instructed on the proper way to address his Wife, apart from her new mistress's irritated "Don't call me ma'am. . . . You're not a Martha" (15). Offred recognizes her, however, as the lead soprano of that television *Gospel Hour* that she watched in childhood. Blonde, petite, increasingly inclined to heavy makeup and runny mascara, deft at squeezing out rapturous tears in mid-hymn, Serena Joy is a parody of televangelistic stars of the 1980s, most vividly evoking Tammy Fay Bakker. "Serena Joy," if we hadn't guessed already, is revealed as her stage name, covering a much more prosaic earlier incarnation, in which she was Pam. The newsmagazine profile that provided that tidbit was discussing her move from singing to speech making, as Serena lectured widely on the sanctity of the home, on the rightness of women staying home. In the new order, literally taken at her word, trapped in her home and "speechless" (44), Serena Joy is neither serene nor joyful. Actually, Offred is uncertain that Serena Joy is still her name, and is the only one to refer to her that way routinely (in her head). Fred (all but once), the servants, and Offred in conversation stick to depersonalized pronouns (she, her), so that in a functional sense she has been unnamed as completely as her Handmaid.

Cora and Rita are too lowly to require name change, but the naming of their category is an ironic detail. It comes from the biblical story (Luke 10.38–42), in which Martha complains bitterly because Mary is sitting listening to and learning from Jesus rather than lending a hand with the housework. Jesus hints gently that the housework is less important than his ministry, which will not last forever (whereas, as almost anyone can testify, housework will definitely last forever). The Son of God applauds Mary's choice of Word over work; the Sons of Jacob prefer (and enforce) Martha's confining herself to work over Word!

In the name game it is significant that Offred's mother and daughter, erased by the regime in all but memory, go nameless, perhaps as part of Offred's strategy to protect them. On the other hand, Moira and Janine, linked to Offred not by blood but by the blood sisterhood of the Handmaids, and physically close at hand, retain their original names; in training at the Red Centre, they continue temporarily to be so addressed by the Aunts and unceasingly so by Offred, even during the period when Janine is Ofwarren, "shorn of her former name" (110). Professor Pieixoto at the end throws these names into doubt, arguing that pseudonyms were probably used by Offred to protect the others should her tapes be captured. But he offers no proof, and seems to base that idea largely on the difficulties he is having researching the names in the tale. He is especially annoyed by the discrepancy between "Serena Joy" and the names of the wives of his two finalists for the position of Commander Fred, so vexed, in fact, that he suggests Offred has been "malicious" in her "invention" of Serena Joy (291). This seems a dubious judgement when one of his alternatives is the equally fluffy "Bambi Mae" (291), and it also indicates a sloppy oversight of Offred's own opinion that Serena Joy is a "stupid name" (43).

The name most open to conjuring is the narrator's. Offred is of course the Handmaid of Fred. But it is hard to pronounce it as concocted, to say Of-Fred; we tend instead to say Off-red, and so she is: a questioner beneath her scarlet garb, a deviant from her training at the Red Centre. And many readers have detected a wordplay on "offered": an offering on the altar of Gilead's agenda; a woman who is capable of offering herself in a romantic relationship despite the institutionalized rape she is suffering; a courageous offerer of counternarratives to her tyrannical society. Michèle Lacombe (7) suggests the intriguing variant "off-read," meaning "mis-read," as she certainly is by Pieixoto, and Patrick Parrinder (20) toys with "Afraid" as another variant both true and untrue of Offred's response to her predicament. In jotting down notes for this study, I soon found myself abbreviating Offred to "O," and that spun off a whole other series of connections: the circles, zeroes, haloes, eggs, and ceiling oval that permeate the text, every one of which invites interpretation. Even several critics' views of the novel (Ableman, Bouson, Kingden, Lehmann-Haupt, Thurman) as partly an erotic or sadomasochistic fantasy, while not readings that worked well for me, tapped into my ruminations with the possible allusion to the S/M classic, *The Story of O*. Offred declares herself a nothing and gravitates to Scrabble words like *zilch* (172), yet in the direst of circumstances is capable of producing a tale with truly global (sic) dimensions.

BODY LANGUAGE

If names seem critical to one's sense of self, there is something even more indispensible for most people: their bodies. In Gilead it is the primary, primal relationship that the new laws have altered. We detect that right from the start, when Offred oddly describes the central blank spot in her ceiling as reminiscent of "the place in a face where the eye has been taken out" (7). Her grasp of physiognomy has become monocular, Cyclopsean, in Gilead, under the influence of the all-seeing Eye. It also lines up with many images of physical dismemberment in the novel, appropriate to a society that classifies its women by bodily parts.

Offred is highly conscious of her changed perspectives on her body. She feels shame in using her female curves to tantalize young Guardians but cannot resist the illusion of power, "power of a dog bone, passive but there" (22). Encountering Japanese tourist women, she is hypnotized by the "blatant" sexuality of their hair, postures, cosmetics, footwear, and skirts (so short to her, discreetly below the knee to us) (27). Attracted and repelled, she reflects on how quickly one's eye adjusts, how soon the new becomes normal, how rapidly one's concepts of modesty can be changed. Ofglen even hides her gloved hands from the eyes of the foreigners (28), although Offred maintains a small pocket of resistance in dismissing as a "line" the official theory — uniting Aunt Lydia with both the most orthodox of Muslims and the most radical of feminists in our time — that to be gazed upon is to be penetrated, violated (28). What distresses her most is the reduction of her significance and value to a single segment of her body, her womb. "I used to think of my body as an instrument, of pleasure, or a means of transportation, or an implement for the accomplishment of my will. . . . There were limits but my body was . . . single, solid, one with me" (69). Now she's a cloud around the all-important uterus, on which new life depends, on which *her* life depends. It is "more real than I am" (69), and she deeply resents that it "determines me so completely" (59), even though she yearns for a pregnancy fully as much as Serena Joy, Cora, and the demographers of Gilead do. Lunching on canned pears (61, 84, 264) and exchanging daily greetings of "Blessed be the fruit" are only two of dozens of coded signals for the womb, "the shape of a pear" (69), through which her monthly moon "transits, pauses, continues on and passes out of sight, and I see despair coming towards me like famine" (69–70). There is an alternative way of reproduction available to her, however, and in her taletelling Offred will modify her creative goal to "a made thing, not something born" (62). By remembering the past, she can re-member the self that Gilead has dismembered.

In a world where sex has been de-eroticized, nature will not be denied. The forbidden and the hidden become erotic, including the mother tongue, the body of language. Reading in the Commander's study becomes orgiastic, frenetic: "If it were eating it would be the gluttony of the famished, if it were sex it would be a swift furtive stand-up in an alley somewhere" (173). Furthermore, with a tip of the hat to Lydia, veiled Muslim women, and radical feminists, she finds that when the Commander watches her read, it is "curiously sexual" and she feels uncomfortably "undressed while he does it" (173).

Her "reduced circumstances" (8) have Offred's senses working overtime. Textures, odours, colours, sounds, tastes real and imagined bombard her. She longs for the "rich dirty cinnamon sigh" of a cigarette (196), and the "smell of nail polish" makes her hungry (28). Walking in Serena's "Tennyson garden, heavy with scent, languid," makes her head swim, makes her think of words like *swoon* (143). It is all part of the unquenchable vitality of living that affirms her existence, "the body's . . . bedrock prayer: *I am, I am*. I am still" (264).

LAST LAUGH

While commentators have had a longstanding preoccupation with the political construct of Gilead, one of the earliest and liveliest essays on the novel concentrated instead on language: Michèle Lacombe's 1986 "The Writing on the Wall: Amputated Speech in Margaret Atwood's *The Handmaid's Tale*." It was an appropriate focus for a novel in which wordplay is so evident and for a republic in which the Word is under lock and key, Scrabble words have become the new eroticism, word litanies keep a desperate woman sane, and "Sign language" (154) has replaced the literacy that was so taken for granted in the time before that Offred herself prepared library books for shredding (162). Offred strives to make words connect, in a linguistic substitute for the physical touch she acutely misses, but at the same time she pulls back from facile word linkages ("The tulips are not tulips of blood, the red smiles are not flowers, neither thing makes a comment on the other" [32]) as cautiously as she does from human ones (opting not to "tempt" Rita with friendship [11], withdrawing from the delicious contact with Nick's boot [77]). Such distinctions and reservations are a matter of control for a woman stripped of power, and also a blow for the individual identities of things ("Each thing is valid and really there" [32]) in a repressive regime that is doing all it can to de-individuate her and all her loved ones. The Commander, an architect of such social homogenization, cannot fathom her insistence that "one and one and one and one" equal "one and one and one and one" (174). By the time she later denies any internal connections in her litany on "chair" (104), we can note the wrongness of that denial (Linda Kauffman, among others, nicely unravels the associations for us [233]) without losing sight of its psychological necessity for her, and we are in a linguistically sensitized position to receive with raised eyebrows Professor Pieixoto's not very funny joke which pivots on the very same word (282).

Which leads us into the question of humour in *The Handmaid's Tale*. "Grim," "humourless," "chilling," "horrifying": you would think from some commentaries that there wasn't a laugh in the novel. Far from it. While sometimes the humour is of the gallows variety, Offred, Moira, and Atwood are here to tell us that wit and laughter are among the best forms not just of self-protective detachment but of resistance to oppression.

The narration of *The Handmaid's Tale* takes its cue from one of the authors Offred reads in the Commander's study, Charles Dickens, whose fiction skilfully alternates dark and light chapters, tragic and comic. Beyond sheer comic relief, the intention is never to leave readers so long in the shadows that they forget the remarkable resilience of the human spirit. In *The Handmaid's Tale* the humour is widely varied: irony, including humorous reversals and incongruity; clever wordplay; subversive obscenities; comic self-denigration; in-jokes; and satire. The profile of humour involves some sharp descents, where halfway through the laugh we land in the deadly serious (e.g., "Two Eyes" jumping from a van but then beating and arresting a citizen), or the reverse, an ascent from a dark situation into a celebration of its comic aspect.

Connections often have been drawn between nations and their characteristic or favourite type of humour. Canada is considered by many to have a special preference for irony, a humorous stance particularly suitable to a country beset by internal tensions of geography, history, language, mythology, and culture, traditionally disinclined and now culturally unable to adopt easily the satisfying but simplistic either/or of traditional satire. To add a second generalization, Atwood is regarded as one of irony's most accomplished contemporary practitioners. Since irony thrives on discrepancies between the real and the ideal, between surface and substance, between the literal and the metaphoric, it is plain that Gilead is a rich ground for the many strains of ironic wit. Incongruities abound in a republic where language has become a minefield and a Kafkaesque paranoia undercuts certainty about everything. If innocent gestures can be fatal, so lethal events can be represented as harmless, as in the ironic effect of Offred's hearing the doorbell being rung by the Eyes coming to arrest her (275) and being whimsically reminded of visits in the time before from cosmetics ladies: "Ding-dong, Avon calling," we remember, despite the gravity of the situation. Sometimes the incongruity touches both the events and the unexpected idiom, as when Offred comes away from the Particicution so hungry "I could eat a horse" (264). And often the irony revolves around the unexpected or reductive similes applied to an action, as when "the Commander fucks, with a regular two-four marching stroke, on and on like a tap dripping. He is preoccupied, like a man humming to himself in the shower without knowing he's humming; like a man who has other things on his mind" (88). And, to turn the tables on Pieixoto, there's a sexual pun on "come" from the ladies: "It's as if he's somewhere else, waiting for himself to come, drumming his fingers on the table while he waits" (88–89). When Fred leaves Serena Joy and Offred, who are still grotesquely locked together in the Ceremonial posture, he closes the door "with exaggerated care behind him, as if both of us are his ailing mother" (89). Even Offred, in a very unfunny situation, remarks, "There's something hilarious about this . . ." (89).

A prime ironic scene involves Offred's discovery that Fred has arranged their illicit and dangerous rendezvous in his study to . . . play Scrabble! Once again, it is all Offred can do to conceal her startled amusement. Her expectations of exotic indulgences or kinky sex in the "forbidden room" stand in absurd contrast to the reality of Scrabble, "once the game of old women, old men, in the summers or in retirement villas," or "of adolescents, once, long long ago," and that descent, what literary theorists call comic reduction, makes her want to "shriek with laughter, fall off my chair" (130). Later, reviewing the Scrabble request in her room, she repeats the reaction she had after the Ceremony: "there's something hilarious about it" (136). She then almost gives vent to the hysterical laughter "boiling like lava in my throat. . . . I'll choke on it. My ribs hurt with holding back, I shake, I heave, seismic, volcanic, I'll burst." But the tone turns from funny to lethal in a split second: "Red all over the cupboard, mirth rhymes with birth, oh to die of laughter." And the fine line between delight and grief is crossed: "I stifle [my laughter] in the folds of the hanging cloak, clench my eyes, from which tears are squeezing" (138).

Unexpected reversals of a different sort are another source of irony throughout the novel. One such is the historical inversion of broadcasts by Radio Free America from Cuba into Gilead (197). Another is the vision of Fred as a perfect figure for "an ad on rural democracy," preserved in a "fly-specked" etching from "some old burned book" (172). Or there is the caption to Offred's imaginings of newly married daughters of the Commanders enduring dull sex by studying dust and spiders on the ceiling: "There's always something to occupy the inquiring mind" (208). And Offred specializes in the silver-lining variety of ironic reversal: repelled by the prospect of holding Serena Joy's wool on a sticky hot day, for example, she takes Pollyanna comfort in the thought that "At least my hands will get lanolined" (191).

A large measure of the humour of *The Handmaid's Tale* comes from one of Offred's survival stratagems, wordplay. Given to etymological musings ever since her days as a librarian, particularly under the influence of Luke, Offred frequently uses linguistic playfulness to elevate her spirits, resist the regime, and pass the time. The machines that print out Soul Scrolls are "Holy Rollers" (156); she experiences "Pen Is Envy" (174) in fingering a forbidden writing implement for the first time in years; sex-starved young Guardians watch the Handmaids "stiffly" as she provocatively swings her hips (22); before Gilead, Labour Day didn't "have anything to do with mothers" (187). She deconstructs Aunt Lydia's description of her "girls" as "pearls" by thinking sardonically that pearls are "congealed oyster spit," a riposte that Lydia unwittingly plays into by continuing, "All of us here will lick you into shape" (108). And my favourite is Offred's fearful fantasy of her meetings with Fred being exposed, which she neutralizes with her facetious "Caught in the act, sinfully Scrabbling. Quick, eat those words" (170).

Although she presents Moira as the one with the razor sense of humour, Offred doesn't need many lessons from her feisty friend on irrepressible irreverence. What she does need is awareness that obscene humour may be effective as a subversive act. It takes some deliberate effort for her to get beyond the decorous behaviour that started in childhood as a reaction to her mother's rowdy, swearing activist friends, and developed into the posture of a conservative, low-profile, law-abiding, easily embarrassed average citizen. She protests to Moira that such crudities do no good, but Moira convinces her otherwise:

75

... she's right, I know that now.... There is something powerful in the whispering of obscenities, about those in power. There's something delightful about it, something naughty, secretive, forbidden, thrilling. It's like a spell, of sorts. It deflates them, reduces them to the common denominator where they can be dealt with. In the paint of the washroom cubicle someone unknown had scratched: *Aunt Lydia sucks*. It was like a flag waved from a hilltop in rebellion. The mere idea of Aunt Lydia doing such a thing was in itself heartening. (208–09)

In some instances the humour works outside of Offred's ken, appreciated only by the reader. Offred's ignorance, if it is fair to call it that, usually serves as a signal that her time before is our time ahead (just a little), as in her bafflement over what we recognize instantly to be Playboy bunny outfits. In that case her puzzlement actually inspires some (to us) ironic questions, on sexual dynamics, that we might not have thought through before. ("[W]hy are rabbits supposed to be sexually attractive to men? How can this bedraggled costume appeal?" [224]). More often, the effect is simpler, as in the amusing reductive intertext of the (in)famous Frederick's of Hollywood catalogues (a boudoir line of women's scanties) in Fred proffering the sequinned, befeathered, garish outfit to Offred to wear to Jezebel's. And here's a macabre one: the name Particicution is "lifted from an exercise program" (289), Pieixoto tells us blandly, but the joke has another grotesque step. Participaction was a Canadian government program geared to rouse couch potatoes from their lethargy; here it's a government program geared to rouse Handmaids (normally forced by the government to be lethargic) to a murderous rage and to participatory execution of dissidents.

At the other end of the humour scale is self-conscious self-deprecation, considered by many a particular Canadian forte. "I never looked good in red, it's not my colour," deadpans Offred (8). "Nothing can be done about my hair," she mock-laments as she prepares for the dangerous excursion to Jezebel's (217). And trying to stir herself to some minimal level of responsiveness to the Commander, she lectures herself, "All you have to do ... is keep your mouth shut and look stupid. It shouldn't be that hard" (221). Some critics (Banerjee, Deer) have objected to the startling disjuncture between this wisecracking voice and the poetic one, but such low-brow, mundane, humorously incongruous comments under the dire circumstances have a serious function; to speak the "normal," everyday way of ordinary times is to suggest that the crazy times are temporary, that normalcy exists and will be restored.

A minor but signature type of humour for Atwood is the inside joke, a small insertion in which she makes fun of some personal detail, sketches a recognizable person, or, like filmmaker Alfred Hitchcock with his trademark cameo appearances, leaves her fingerprint on the text. Examples include Commander Fred's having been a market researcher before Gilead, as was Atwood for a time in the 1960s. Another is the romantic inscription Offred finds still carved into the school desks at the Red Centre: "*M. loves G., 1972*" (107), alluding to Atwood's relationship with novelist Graeme Gibson. In other novels such as *Lady Oracle*, this humorous impulse operates as a full-scale roman à clef, wherein real people appear in thin disguises, identifiable, usually comically so. Here, in *The Handmaid's Tale*, the in-jokes are few, but are moments where Atwood steps out briefly from behind her creation; they may also be occasions when Atwood reminds us that her fictional "time before" is just ahead of a real time which she and we inhabit.

At three points in the novel, an apparent joke is significantly rejected. In one, Offred compares Serena Joy's muffled weeping to "a fart in church" (85), which everyone pretends not to notice; aware she is talking about real pain and unwilling to make it the butt (as it were!) of nervous adolescent humour at the same time that she wants to convey the level of tension, she admits, "I feel, as always, the urge to laugh, but not because I think it's funny" (85). On another occasion, regarding the requirement that Handmaids keep their hair long and covered, "Aunt Lydia said: Saint Paul said it's either that or a close shave. She laughed, that held-back neighing of hers, as if she'd told a joke" (58). Offred's unamused reaction demonstrates some basic principles of humour: unless you're telling it yourself, it's a lot less funny if the joke is at your expense, if it's your neck that will feel Gilead's close shave. The last of the trilogy of unjokes involves a saying Offred's mother had been fond of, repeated by Moira after the coup had crushed women's rights: "It's you and me up against the wall, baby"; Offred remembers the moment, adding, ". . . she wasn't intending to be funny" (163). The Wall is perhaps the landmark of humour's limits, now that we've entered Gilead, and in humour, as any entertainer will tell you, context is all.

POSTSCRIPT

Asked by Nancy Gage whether her purpose in *The Handmaid's Tale* was "to warn," Atwood answered in a characteristically circuitous way:

> Let me put it this way: If you see somebody walking toward a large hole in the ground and you want them to fall into it, you don't say anything. I don't know whether you saw *Time* magazine a few weeks ago. It had on the cover "Politics, Religion, and Money." And it was about the potential presidential nomination bid that the evangelical right is making in 1988. If I were an inhabitant of this country, I would be worried about the low voting rate. That means that 25, 26, 27 percent is controlling the rest.

This analysis gives specifics and statistics to a generalization she had made in a 1980 essay called "Witches": "If we cease to judge this world, we may find ourselves, very quickly, in one which is infinitely worse" (*Second Words* 333). It *is* a warning, then, of the dangers of absolutist and elitist thought, and the even greater danger of not paying attention, embedded in a riveting tale, marvellously constructed and poetically executed.

Has the message got through? Yes. And no. Has the artistry of the message been detected? No. And yes. Revolutionary Russian novelist Eugene Ivanovich Zamiatin could have been referring to *The Handmaid's Tale* in his definition of a good book: "There are books of the same chemical composition as dynamite. The difference lies only in the fact that one stick of dynamite explodes once, but one book explodes thousands of times" (xi). Listen to some of the ongoing explosions.

> Atwood has successfully aroused the reader's conscience, implying that the future rests upon the responsible choice and subsequent action of the individual. (Herridge 38)

> . . . the novel achieves what it is meant to do, shatters complacency and pulls us up short. (Holliday)

> The reader who is swept up into the story must stand back from it to realize its fundamental absurdity. (Dooley)

. . . the power of the book comes not from Atwood's inspired flights of fancy or felicities of style but from her deliberate subjugation of imagination to demonstrable fact. (Kendall 2)

All of this is woven into a complex and witty novel that is alternately funny and frightening precisely because it is so plausible. (Sussman)

Atwood's "what ifs" are so lacking plausibility or inevitability as to be embarrassing. (Flower 318)

A rare emotional range and intellectual soundness, linked to a concern with global issues. (Tilley 9)

The brilliance of Atwood's novel, and the novel is truly brilliant, rests in her creation of a future that is a too logical extension of many dimensions of the present. (Staines)

. . . *The Handmaid's Tale* is entirely dependent on this [wildly implausible] assumption of imminent widespread genetic failure. (Davis)

. . . Atwood, like any good writer, has chosen to write to an audience of human beings who have their own minds to think with and their own hearts to feel with and who are psychologically healthy enough to grasp what is being unfolded to them. (Kilodney 32)

It is precisely that documentary approach — and the gritty realism of the actions and conversations reported — that gives "The Handmaid's Tale" its uncanny air of believability. (Roberson)

Ms. Atwood's future is not only unlikely but rather uninteresting. (Ableman 35)

Atwood is a forceful writer and brilliantly conveys the horror and boredom of captivity. (Waugh 91)

. . . in its very essence, *The Handmaid's Tale* is vivid and immediate. (Tyler)

. . . she gives us far too little action and far too much of the *longueurs* long suffered by the interned Offred. . . . (Cheuse)

This is a witty, angry piece of writing. As a novel of ideas it is provocative and ingenious and as an adventure . . . it is narrated with pace and nerve. (Cooke)

[Offred's] tale, in Atwood's masterful hands, is extraordinarily satisfying, disturbing and compelling. (Johnson 2)

Her writing . . . has the energy and clarity of a swift river. It is limpid without being limp; clever without being silly; controlled without being stilted; precise without being pedantic. (Stimpson 766)

The Handmaid's Tale brings out the very best in Atwood — moral vision, biting humor and a poet's imagination (Jackson)

. . . it is powerless to scare. . . . it lacks imagination. . . . (McCarthy 35)

. . . Atwood's [book is suffused] by life — the heroine's irrepressible vitality and the author's lovely subversive hymn to our ordinary life, as lived, amid perils and pollution, now. (Updike 123)

The Handmaid's Tale is not a perfect work, yet any flaws are minor ones in comparison with the impact of the novel as a whole. (Heger)

By choosing as the central character a woman who, with or without autonomy, does not identify with victims and cares only about a man's love, Atwood warns how a Dystopia for women could succeed. (Kane 10)

. . . the portrait of the national situation [in Gilead] is skimpy, the international almost nonexistent. Moreover, there is little reference to industry. (O'Brien 252)

Atwood's novel is a work of literature, not a philosophical or scientific treatise. (Peers)

. . . *The Handmaid's Tale* provides a compelling lesson in power politics and in reasonable intentions gone hysteric. (Rosenberg P8)

. . . as a serious study of humanity's ills, as a diagnostic novel, it is Canlit's most overpraised imposture. (Kingden 32)

Elizabeth Kingden gave Margaret Atwood a back-handed compliment by using *The Handmaid's Tale* as a starting point for a discussion of real-life problems. (Wain)

This haunting and often very moving book shows us our world in a glass darkly. (Jolley 26)

Canadian lady novelists evidently harbor peculiar misconceptions about the New Right's idea of religious observance. (Thompson 440)

Margaret Atwood's terrain is sexual politics only, and within it, she strikes out on a broad front, not just against Right-to-Lifers, anti-ERA campaigners, born-again Christians, and Stepford Wives, but also against feminist puritans . . . and essentialists who hymn childbirth, menarche, and sisterhood. (Warner)

She is a rare and splendid talent, and every intelligent and patriotic American — especially the American Atheist — should be grateful to her. (Brodhead 48)

Atwood seems both too sure she knows what she means and too anxious for us to get her *right*. (Thurman 108)

She seems to leave more room than most authors do for the reader to participate, to wonder, ponder, fill in the blanks . . . (Hartman)

Atwood's story, told with her usual wicked irony, is far-fetched but not impossible and plays brilliantly on niggling feminist doubts. (Ingoldby 31)

[A convincing dystopia requires] an unremitting flood of lurid and grotesque imagery such as the largely inarticulate and undiscerning Offred manages to summon up only rarely. (Linkous 6)

Her sinewy style is not only pleasing but also shows her to be an agile theorist, dissecting conventional sexual roles without lapsing into apology or its opposite extreme, bitchiness. (Adler 72)

Even more terrifying is the lesson the novel holds. There is little to support the belief that human beings cannot break down, cannot be crushed. (Jaidev)

In the end, apparently, Atwood can come up with nothing more hopeful and energetic than the well-worn Canadian motto: "It could be worse." (Thomas)

Gripping like an intelligent thriller, compelling like all believable dystopias, it's also a reply to puritans of left and right, showing how, even in conditions of dire psychic deprivation, people still want and get sex. It's a sign of life, indestructible. (Dick 31)

In The Handmaid's Tale, Atwood's pessimism comes to the fore as she attempts to frighten us into an awareness of our destiny before it's too late. (French)

No critical position is taken on this novel that is not energetically challenged by another. That is somehow appropriate in the face of a novelist who distrusts closure, a central narrative that refuses to provide an ending, and an epilogue that wraps up its speculations with a question. Expected to provide a "Conclusion" to my introduction to *The Handmaid's Tale*, I have found it less presumptuous to offer this multivocal, highly contentious "Postscript." To those voices I add my own, inevitably personal perspective (which is all any critic really does, no matter what Professor Pieixoto might try to argue about objectivity). That perspective — no surprise in someone who has taken the time to write a reader's guide — is highly positive. A last look at the prose may help explain.

Consider this passage:

The knock would come at the door
I'd open, with relief, desire
He was so momentary, so condensed
And yet there seemed no end to him
We would lie in those afternoon beds,
afterwards, hands on each other
talking it over
Possible, impossible.
What could be done?
We thought we had such problems.
How were we to know we were happy?

This is my "poetic" transcription of a randomly selected passage of prose (48) from *The Handmaid's Tale*. It is one way of illustrating the extraordinary degree to which Atwood blurs the line between genres, creating fiction that is as lyrically "poetic" as her poetry is tensely "prosaic." A socially cautionary tale that I find alarmingly credible, the novel is successfully suspenseful, vivid, and peopled by compelling characters. But for me, it is above all that skilled intersection of genres, and the rich, involving text that results, that is the crowning achievement of *The Handmaid's Tale*. With her intense delivery of powerful content in a seemingly plain but infinitely complex style, Atwood obliges me to become engaged in her Gilead and to deny none of it.

Works Cited

Ableman, Paul. "After the Revolution." *Literary Review* 94 (April 1986): 35–36.
British reviewer finds the novel unconvincing, uninteresting, lacking (as he says all female writing does!) in technological intricacy. Sees no current analogues. Finds humour only in "Historical Notes."

Adachi, Ken. "Atwood Takes a Chance and Wins." *Toronto Star* 13 Oct. 1985: E1.
Interview, discussing historical and other aspects of the novel.

Adler, Constance. "Canadian Club." *Philadelphia Magazine* 77.3 (1986): 67, 71–72.
Sees Atwood and other Canadian novelists as worried about trends in U.S. Admires understatement as "perfect for the cautionary nature" (71) of the novel and applauds the relevance to current abuses of power.

Andriano, Joseph. "*The Handmaid's Tale* as Scrabble game." *Essays on Canadian Writing* 48 (Winter 1993): 89–96.
Argues that Scrabble is a figure for the whole novel, a game of gaining an advantage with words, counteraction, crossing, text and countertext, word power.

Armbruster, Jane. "Memory and Politics: A Reflection on *The Handmaid's Tale* by Margaret Atwood." *Social Justice* 173 (Fall 1990): 146.
Considers our culture Gileadean in many ways, privileging head values (rational, masculine) over heart values (emotional, feminine). Textual commentary plus personal manifesto.

Atwood, Margaret. *Alias Grace*. Toronto: McClelland and Stewart, 1996.

___. The Animals in That Country. Toronto: Oxford UP, 1968.

___, and Joyce Barkhouse. *Anna's Pet*. Toronto: Lorimer, 1980.

___. *Bluebeard's Egg*. Toronto: McClelland, 1983.

___. *Bodily Harm*. Toronto: McClelland, 1981.

___, ed. *The Canlit Foodbook*. Toronto: Totem, 1987.

___. *Cat's Eye*. Toronto: McClelland, 1988.

___. *The Circle Game*. Toronto: Contact, 1966.

___. *Dancing Girls and Other Stories*. Toronto: McClelland, 1977.

___. *Days of the Rebels: 1815–1840*. Canada's Illustrated Heritage Series. Toronto: Natural Science of Canada, 1977.

___. *Double Persephone*. Toronto: Hawkshead, 1961.

___. *The Edible Woman*. Toronto: McClelland, 1969.

___. *For the Birds*. Toronto: Douglas, 1990.

___. *Good Bones*. Toronto: Coach House, 1992.

___. *Good Bones and Simple Murders*. Toronto: Talese/Doubleday, 1993.

___. *The Handmaid's Tale*. 1985. Toronto: Seal, 1986.

___. *Interlunar*. Toronto: Oxford UP, 1984.

___. "Interview with Margaret Atwood." With Beryl Donaldson Langer. *Australian-Canadian Studies* 6.1 (1988): 125–36.

___. "An Interview with Margaret Atwood." With Sue Matheson. *Herizons* Jan./Feb. 1986: 20–22.

Winnipeg interview involves close discussion of the novel.

___. *The Journals of Susanna Moodie*. Toronto: Oxford UP, 1970.

___. *Lady Oracle*. Toronto: McClelland, 1976.

___. *Life before Man*. Toronto: McClelland, 1979.

___. Margaret Atwood Papers. Thomas Fisher Rare Book Library, U of Toronto.

___. *Morning in the Burned House*. Toronto: McClelland, 1995.

___. *Murder in the Dark: Short Fictions and Prose Poems*. Toronto: Coach House, 1983.

___, ed. *The New Oxford Book of Canadian Verse in English*. Toronto: Oxford UP, 1982.

___, and Robert Weaver, eds. *The Oxford Book of Canadian Short Stories in English*. Toronto: Oxford UP, 1986.

___, and Barry Callaghan, eds. and introd. *The Poetry of Gwendolyn MacEwen, Vol. One: The Early Years*. 1992. *Vol. Two: The Later Years*. 1993.

___. *Power Politics*. Toronto: Anansi, 1971.

___. *Procedures for Underground*. Toronto: Oxford UP, 1970.

___. "Q&Q Interview: Margaret Atwood." With Katherine Govier. *Quill & Quire* Sept. 1985: 66–67.

A rewarding interview in which Atwood discusses dystopia versus science fiction; optimism, politics, men, and stylistics in the novel; Offred's relations with her mother; historical analogues; treatment of women; and writing.

___. *The Robber Bride*. Toronto: McClelland, 1993.

___. *Second Words: Selected Critical Prose*. Toronto: Anansi, 1982.

___. *Selected Poems*. Toronto: Oxford UP, 1976.

___. *Selected Poems II: Poems Selected and New, 1976–1986*. Toronto: Oxford UP, 1986.

___. *Selected Poems: 1966–1984*. Toronto: Oxford UP, 1990.

___. *Strange Things: The Malevolent North in Canadian Literature*. New York: Oxford UP, 1995.

___. *Surfacing*. Toronto: McClelland, 1972.

___. *Survival: A Thematic Guide to Canadian Literature*. Toronto: Anansi, 1972.

___. "Tightrope-Walking over Niagara Falls." With Geoff Hancock. *Margaret Atwood: Conversations*. Ed. Earl G. Ingersoll. Willowdale, ON: Firefly, 1990. 191–220.

A wide-ranging, plain-talking interview conducted in 1986 in Toronto.

___. *True Stories*. Toronto: Oxford UP, 1981.

___. *Two-Headed Poems*. Toronto: Oxford UP, 1978.

___. *Up in the Tree*. Toronto: McClelland, 1978.

___. *Wilderness Tips*. Toronto: McClelland, 1991.

___. *You Are Happy*. Toronto: Oxford UP, 1974.

Baccolini, Raffaella. "Breaking the Boundaries: Gender, Genre, and Dystopia." *Per una definizione dell'utopia: Metodologie e discipline a confronto*. Ed. Nadia Minerva. Ravenna: Longo, 1992. 137–46.

Reviews traditional dystopia and argues Atwood has transformed the genre, using language, creativity, openendedness, and Offred's fluid identity.

Banerjee, Chinmoy. "Alice in Disneyland: Criticism as Commodity in *The Handmaid's Tale*." *Essays on Canadian Writing* 41 (Summer 1990): 74–92.

Sees the novel as historically shallow, improbable, underdeveloped, not a dystopia but rather "a costume Gothic projected against a dystopian setting" (83). Disputes at length the two separate(d) voices of Offred: one witty, allusive, and sophisticated; the other chatty, redundant, naive.

Bartkowski, Frances. *Feminist Utopias*. Lincoln: U of Nebraska P, 1989.

Chapter 5 compares *The Handmaid's Tale* with Louky Bersianik's *The Eugelionne* (1976). Sees the *Tale* as the start of dystopias, when the optimism of the 1970s fades into the antifeminist backlash of the 1980s. Stereotypes of light as knowledge and darkness as ignorance are disrupted in the novel, with the Night chapters showing different ways of knowing and resisting.

Battiata, Mary. "Atwood's Nightmare New World: The Canadian Writer and Her Cautionary Tale of the Future." *Washington Post*. 6 Apr. 1986: G1, G6.

Part report, part interview discussing sources and aspects of the novel.

Bazin, Nancy Topping. "Women and Revolution in Dystopian Fiction: Nadine Gordimer's *July's People* and Margaret Atwood's *The Handmaid's Tale*." *Selected Essays: International Conference on Representing Revolution 1989*. Ed. John Michael Crafton. Carrollton, GA: West Georgia College, 1991. 115–27.

Sees both novels as dystopian, by writers committed (albeit reluctantly) to the view that the personal is political, both showing the price of remaining disengaged or unalert to all encroachments upon freedom, whether from the right, the left, or academe.

Bergmann, Harriet F. " 'Teaching Them to Read': A Fishing Expedition in *The Handmaid's Tale*." *College English* 51.8 (Dec. 1989): 847–54.

Regards language and its control as the key components of the novel. Includes a trenchant analysis of the "Historical Notes."

Black, Larry. "Of Atwood and the U.S. Glitterati." *Vancouver Sun* 22 Feb. 1986: D4.

Counters Mary McCarthy's negative review, arguing the plausibility of a coup in a country with a tradition of revolution and a belief in overnight change.

Bouson, J. Brooks. *Brutal Choreographies: Oppositional Strategies and Narrative Design in the Novels of Margaret Atwood*. Amherst, MA: U of Massachusetts P, 1993.

Uses feminist and psychoanalytic theory to investigate aspects of structure, gender and power politics, romance, and rhetoric in the novel.

Bradbury, Ray. *Fahrenheit 451*. 1953. New York: Simon, 1967.

The dystopian story of one man's seemingly futile resistance to a totalitarian state he originally served by burning books.

Brodhead, James E. Rev. of *The Handmaid's Tale*. *American Atheist* 28.7 (July 1986): 45, 48.

Positive review in a Texan journal, citing many historical analogues, especially the blurring of church and state in current American events, and admiring Offred.

Burack, Cynthia. "Bringing Women's Studies to Political Science: The Handmaid in the Classroom." *NWSA Journal* 1.2 (Winter 1988–89): 274–83.

Combines feminist textual readings and pedagogic guidelines to show how to challenge and expand political science students' definitions of the political.

Burgess, Anthony. *A Clockwork Orange*. 1962. New York: Norton, 1963.

A famous dystopian novel in which a future state is terrorized by teenage gangs speaking a hybrid language called Nadsat.

Buss, Helen M. "Maternality and Narrative Strategies in the Novels of Margaret Atwood." *Atlantis* 15.1 (Fall 1989): 76–83.

Investigates Atwood's "vision of femaleness" (77) in seven novels, including *The Handmaid's Tale*, and sees the "constant lesson" (81) of the novel as a caution against hiding in the personal, uninvolved and therefore powerless in the publically political.

Caldwell, Larry W. "Wells, Orwell, and Atwood: (EPI)Logic and Eu/Utopia." *Extrapolation: A Journal of Science Fiction and Fantasy* 33.4 (Winter 1992): 333–45.

Traces the novel's debt to Wells and Orwell and its categorization as a real utopia, wherein the narrator is equivocal and there is an unresolved no/where-now/here polarity.

Cheuse, Alan. "Margaret Atwood Stumbles on Science Fiction." *USA Today* 7 Feb. 1986: 4D. Hostile review that calls the story "disappointing" and "boring," having "far too little action" and constructed on a "weird theocracy."

Conboy, Sheila C. "Scripted, Conscripted, and Circumscribed: Body Language in Margaret Atwood's *The Handmaid's Tale*." *Anxious Power: Reading, Writing, and Ambivalence in Narrative by Women*. Ed. Carol J. Singley and Susan Elizabeth Sweeney. Albany: State U of New York P, 1993. 349–62.

Traces Offred's ambivalence about "liberating her own body from the burden of other people's texts and representing her text as body" (350) and detects a parallel doubtfulness in Atwood about women's ability in a still-sexist future to control their own narratives.

C[ooke], J[udith]. "New in Hardback." *Fiction Magazine* 5.2 (Spring 1986): 2.

Positive British review suggesting that the men of Gilead "have something in common with the heroes of [the TV series] Dallas."

Cooke, Nathalie. "The Politics of Ventriloquism: Margaret Atwood's Fictive Confessions." *Various Atwoods: Essays on the Later Poems, Short Fiction, and Novels*. Ed. Lorraine York. Concord, ON: Anansi, 1995. 207–28.

Explores the strategies, duplicities, and implications of the confessions of Offred, as well as *Lady Oracle*'s Joan and *Cat's Eye*'s Elaine.

Culp, Kris. "Reconstructing the Church: 'The Handywoman's Tale.'" *Criterion* 26.3 (Autumn 1987): 9, 12.

Uses the novel as inspiration for a call to action in aid of "feminist redemptive community" (12) in the Christian faith.

Davidson, Arnold E. "Future Tense: Making History in *The Handmaid's Tale*." VanSpanckeren and Castro 113–21.

Starts from the premise that "How we *choose* to construct history partly determines the history we are likely to get" (115), moving into an indictment of the "Historical Notes" as a metahistory of patriarchy.

Davidson, Cathy N. "A Feminist '1984': Margaret Atwood Talks about Her Exciting New Novel." *Ms* Feb. 1986: 24–26.

Partly an interview, with framing commentary judging the novel Atwood's best yet. Compares and contrasts Atwood with Huxley and Orwell. Admires the gripping suspense; sees Offred as a latter-day Anne Frank.

Davis, Robert I. "Stereotypical, Tedious." *Tribune Review* [Greensburgh, PA] 13 Apr. 1986: C8.

Finds the novel "wildly implausible" and "dreary," the characters "unamusing" and "stereotypic."

Deer, Glenn. *Postmodern Canadian Fiction and the Rhetoric of Authority*. Montreal: McGill-Queen's UP, 1994.

Argues, with extensive textual detail, that Atwood's skill as a storyteller intrudes and manipulates, that Offred's narration is too sophisticated and artful for us to believe her self-presentation as an innocent, bumbling recorder. Is disturbed by Offred's interest in power and ambivalence about evil, and by Atwood's implicit reduction of bleak social criticism via romance rhetoric to mere entertainment.

Dick, Leslie. Rev. of *The Handmaid's Tale*. *New Statesman* 114 (17 July 1987): 31.

Short admiring British review, arguing that Atwood is celebrating the impossibility of "rul[ing] desire by decree."

Dooley, D.J. Rev. of *The Handmaid's Tale*. *Canadian Churchman* 112.2 (Feb. 1986): 25.

Finds the story "gripping" and "clever" but fundamentally absurd and anti-religion.

Doud, Katherine. "A Woman's Place: Future." *Kalamazoo Gazette* 15 Feb. 1987: G1, G2.

A review which settles for summary over evaluation, but seems to support the novel being a plausible warning, maybe even a forecast. Typical of many reviews in the surprising errors in plot summary.

Dudar, Helen. "No Balm in Atwood's Gilead." *Wall Street Journal* 12 Feb. 1986: 28.

Finds the novel "mesmerizing, manipulative, scary and, for female readers, sometimes viscerally painful." Sees Atwood as that rare writer who can render a story "in a mood at once bereaved and witty."

Ehrenreich, Barbara. "Feminism's Phantoms." *New Republic* 17 Mar. 1986: 33–35.

Ambivalent, fascinating review, seeing the novel as a "fantasy of regression" involving Offred's and the reader's "deepening masochism" and criticizing the dystopia as thinly textured (34). Detects a warning about repressive impulses not just in the religious right but also in feminism.

Evans, Mark. "Versions of History: *The Handmaid's Tale* and Its Dedicatees." *Margaret Atwood: Writing and Subjectivity: New Critical Essays*. Ed. Colin Nicholson. New York: St. Martin's, 1994. 177–88.

An interesting study of the connections of Mary Webster and Perry Miller to the novel dedicated to them.

Ferns, Chris. "The Value/s of Dystopia: *The Handmaid's Tale* and the Anti-Utopian Tradition." *Dalhousie Review* 69.3 (Fall 1989): 373–82.

Compares and contrasts the novel with Zamiatin's *We*, Huxley's *Brave New World*, and Orwell's *Nineteen Eighty-Four*, finding those dystopian classics anti-female, and defining seven Atwood deviations from the male dystopian tradition, primarily involving subversive strategies of humour, evasion, self-assertion, and survival.

Filipczak, Dorota. "Is There No Balm in Gilead?: Biblical Intertext in *The Handmaid's Tale*." *Literature & Theology* 7.2 (June 1993): 171–85.

Documents the demonic misrepresentation of Judeo-Christian religion that is Gilead, using close biblical comparisons.

Finnell, Susanna. "Unwriting the Quest: Margaret Atwood's Fiction and *The Handmaid's Tale*." *Women and the Journey: The Female Travel Experience*. Ed. Bonnie Frederick and Susan H. McLeod. Pullman, WA: Washington State UP, 1993. 199–215.

A scattered discussion of the novel, but offers the interesting perspective that Offred's capitulation is the precise start of an "anti-quest," the goal of which is to be "saved rather than an exercise of the fighting will" (204); this anti-quest journey will be an enigma, invisible in the gap between her final words and the "Historical Notes."

Fitting, Peter. "The Turn from Utopia in Recent Feminist Fiction." *Feminism, Utopia, and Narrative*. Ed. Libby Falk Jones and Sarah Webster Goodwin. Tennessee Studies in Literature 32. Knoxville: U of Tennessee P, 1990. 141–58.

Criticizes the "Historical Notes" as a mechanism that "tells the reader not to worry" (151) but defends Atwood's not inventing the newspeak that reviewer McCarthy wanted. Candidly longs for the utopias of the 1960s and 1970s but is glad Atwood and other dystopians (Elgin, Fairbairn, LeGuin) are there to warn us against complacency.

Flower, Dean. "Fables of Identity." *Hudson Review* 39 (Summer 1986): 318–20.

Rejects the novel as an implausible "fizzle" which hides Atwood's "natural sarcastic wit" under a "solemn nightmare" in which the only politics is sexual. Concedes that the narrative is skilful, "human and disturbing — if you can forget about the absurdity" (318).

Foley, Michael. " 'Basic Victim Positions' and the Women in Margaret Atwood's *The Handmaid's Tale*." *Atlantis* 15.2 (Spring 1990): 50–58.

Uses Atwood's victim posture construct from *Survival* to categorize the women of the novel, seeing Offred shuttling among positions but eventually triumphing in #4 through telling her tale.

___. "Satiric Intent in the 'Historical Notes' Epilogue of Margaret Atwood's *The Handmaid's Tale*." *Commonwealth* 11.2 (Spring 1989): 44–52.

In a close study of the Notes, sees Atwood warning us of the perennial danger of morally and intellectually bankrupt ideas even in the university.

Freibert, Lucy M. "Control and Creativity: The Politics of Risk in Margaret Atwood's *The Handmaid's Tale*." *Critical Essays on Margaret Atwood*. Ed. Judith McCombs. Boston: Hall, 1988. 280–91.

A close and useful analysis of the book, with an indictment of the post-Gilead society of 2195.

French, William. "Pessimistic Future." *Globe and Mail* 5 Oct. 1985: D18.

Sees the novel as a partly successful "sermon" that tries to scare us into awareness of too many dark futures at once. Views the "Historical Notes" as a "whimsical postscript" and takes Atwood's message to be that the present with all its flaws is preferable to a "future without freedom."

Gage, Nancy. "Talking with Margaret Atwood about *The Handmaid's Tale*." *Impact* [Albuquerque *Journal Magazine*] 15 Apr. 1986: 10.

Five interview questions appended to a favourable review.

Garrett-Petts, W.F. "Reading, Writing, and the Postmodern Condition: Interpreting Margaret Atwood's *The Handmaid's Tale*." *Open Letter* 7th ser. 1 (Spring 1988): 74–92.

Argues that Atwood, dedicated to didactic goals, wants us to see connections between the text and our own world, to go through and beyond process (the focus of postmodernists) to the political. Believes Offred exists only as a speaking voice, whose narrative but not whose self is reconstructed by the reader.

Givner, Jessie. "Names, Faces and Signatures in Margaret Atwood's *Cat's Eye* and *The Handmaid's Tale*." *Canadian Literature* 133 (Summer 1992): 56–75.

Challenges the popular view of Atwood as preoccupied with binary oppositions when she actually "disrupts" (56) boundaries and polarities, especially between autobiography and fiction, above all in *Cat's Eye* and *The Handmaid's Tale*.

Glendinning, Victoria. "Lady Oracle." *Saturday Night* Jan. 1986: 39–41.

Part review, part Atwood profile, finding the novel "disturbingly believable" and full of familiar Atwood themes. Sees Atwood as increasingly hobbled by the self-consciousness that often results from fame.

Goddard, John. "Profile: Lady Oracle." *Books in Canada* Nov. 1985: 6–8, 10.

Profile of and interview with Atwood, who resists his attempts to pin down a moral/feminist message, insisting she is looking at patterns and workings of power structures, not passing judgements.

Gotsch-Thomson, Susan. "The Integration of Gender into the Teaching of Classical Social Theory: Help from *The Handmaid's Tale*." *Teaching Sociology* 18 (Jan. 1990): 69–73.

An account of using the novel in a social theory class to illuminate Marx, Durkheim, Goffman, Gilman, Weber, Mead, etc., and to help students apply those theories to contemporary situations.

Greer, Germaine. *Sex and Destiny: The Politics of Human Fertility*. New York: Harper, 1984.

Source for a discarded epigraph; research resource for the novel.

Halliday, David. "On Atwood." *Waves* 15.4 (Spring 1987): 51–54.

A caustic, jealous review by an obscure writer, rejecting everything about the novel.

Hammer, Stephanie Barbé. "The World as It Will Be? Female Satire and the Technology of Power in *The Handmaid's Tale*." *Modern Fiction Studies* 20.2 (Spring 1990): 39–49.

Considers the novel a successful appropriation of a traditionally male genre, satire, for feminist purposes, using multiple targets which include sexism and women's complicity in "the insidious disciplinary mechanisms of contemporary society" (46).

Hansen, Elaine Tuttle. "Mothers Tomorrow and Mothers Yesterday, but Never Mothers Today." *Narrating Mothers: Theorizing Maternal Subjectivities*. Ed. Brenda O. Daly and Maureen T. Reddy. Knoxville: U of Tennessee P, 1991. 21–43.

A comparative reading of Marge Piercy's utopian *Woman on the Edge of Time* and Atwood's dystopian *The Handmaid's Tale*, investigating both motherhood and the inability to mother, specifically focusing on the tragic loss of a girlchild.

Hartman, Diane. "Male Chauvinism Is Big Brother in an Engrossing Tale." *Denver Post* 23 Feb. 1986: D19.

Review praising the style, premise, and pace of the novel.

Heger, Teresa. "Atwood Fashions Another Feminist Novel." *Daily Iowan* [Iowa City] 24 Apr. 1986: 8B.

Review detecting only minor flaws in a novel seen as a departure for Atwood, "combining the mundane . . . with the unbelievable," but featuring recurrent Atwood themes.

Hengen, Shannon. *Margaret Atwood's Power: Mirrors, Reflections and Images in Select Fiction and Poetry*. Toronto: Second Story, 1993.

Argues the novel is an indictment of "regressive narcissism as it has affected American feminists" and sees the gender of characters as starting with this novel to "matter less to Atwood" than their capacity to question and undermine the established order (99).

Herridge, Catherine. "Make No Assumptions." *Harvard Advocate* 120.1 (Dec. 1986): 37–38.

Review admiring the prose and relevance, seeing Atwood's central concerns as the quandary between freedom to and freedom from, the falseness of assumptions about human progress, and the responsibility of the individual.

Holliday, Barbara. "A Blunt Portrait of Women's Primal Fear." *Detroit Free Press* 26 Jan. 1986: 9E.

Review admiring Offred's "intelligent voice," the poetic intensity, and the "brilliant and Machiavellian" way the plot unfolds. One playful quibble on the impossibility of machine-gunning Congress "in one fell swoop . . . given that body's notorious attendance record."

Howells, Coral Ann. *Private and Fictional Words: Canadian Women Novelists of the 1970s and 1980s*. London: Methuen, 1987. 53–70.

Chapter 3, devoted to *Bodily Harm* and *The Handmaid's Tale*, identifies a "politics of survival" (70) in Offred's alternative powers of "Forgiveness, love and trust" (68).

Huxley, Aldous. *Brave New World*. London: Chatto, 1932.

A classic dystopia, presenting a satirical picture of a future world in which science claims to have solved all human problems.

Ingoldby, Grace. "Lives of Quiet Despair." *New Statesman* 28 Mar. 1986: 30–31.

Brief, approving British review, seeing the premise as unlikely but possible, the delivery brilliantly ironic. Foregrounds a flashback in the novel which exposes women's capacity to blame themselves when things go wrong.

Jackson, Marni. "Critic's Choice: Margaret Atwood Writes a Brilliant Fable about the Future." *Chatelaine* Oct. 1985: 8.

Canadian reviewer finds the scenario "alarmingly close to home."

Jaidev. "Into the Motherland." *Times of India* [New Delhi] 29 Nov. 1987, Sunday review section: 4.

Review admires the "clinical, chilled prose" and Atwood's contribution of a new dystopian theme to the genre: woman as commodity, directly derived from "present-day realities."

Johnson, Joyce. "Margaret Atwood's Brave New World." *Washington Post* 2 Feb. 1986: 1–2.

Highly positive review, praising especially the undoctrinaire subtleties of the sexual politics, the warning against passivity, and the balancing of human and ideological. Sees the novel as taking a new fictional direction in a time of too much fiction about privileged, solipsistic concerns.

Jolley, Elizabeth. "A World without Love." CRNLE *Reviews Journal* [Australia] 1 (1987): 23–26.

Famous fiction writer cites historical and current analogues but dismisses any need for realistic details in a novel she finds "a brilliant and frightening picture of a world without love" (26).

Jones, Dorothy. "Not Much Balm in Gilead." *Commonwealth* 11.2 (Spring 1989): 31–43.

A general discussion of the novel, with special attention to imagery and symbolism.

Kaler, Anne K. " 'A Sister, dipped in blood': Satiric Inversion of the Formation Techniques of Women Religious in Margaret Atwood's Novel *The Handmaid's Tale*." *Christianity and Literature* 38.2 (Winter 1989): 43–62.

Studies in detail the novel's inversion of characteristics of nuns and their training as well as biblical references and religious imagery. Uses "satiric" and "ironic" interchangeably.

Kane, Patricia. "A Woman's Dystopia: Margaret Atwood's *The Handmaid's Tale*." *Notes on Contemporary Literature* 185 (Nov. 1988): 9–10.

Review approving the novel but severely condemning Offred for her selfish focus on her own survival, lack of compassion for Janine, and caring "only about a man's love" (10). In giving Offred those flaws, Atwood shows how feasible a dystopia for women is.

Kauffman, Linda. "Special Delivery: Twenty-first Century Epistolarity in *The Handmaid's Tale*." *Writing the Female Voice: Essays on Epistolary Literature*. Ed. Elizabeth Goldsmith. Boston: Northeastern UP, 1989. 221–44.

Detailed inquiry into Offred's narration, with wide-ranging corollary points from politics to imagery. Sees Offred as a heroine to the end, delivering a "defiant testimony" (241).

Kendall, Elaine. "A Chilling Portrait of What May Be." *Los Angeles Times*, 9 Feb. 1986 book review section: 1–2.

Positive review, seeing Gilead as "firmly based upon actuality" but musing that a male reviewer might be more ambivalent. Thinks Atwood's nationality gives her the advantage of being "close enough for involvement, sufficiently removed for perspective." Calls the "Historical Notes" a "desperately needed and hilarious spoof."

Ketterer, David. "Margaret Atwood's *The Handmaid's Tale*: A Contextual Dystopia." *Science-Fiction Studies* 16 (1989): 209–17.

Distinguishes the novel from the dystopian tradition in that it moves not linearly but cyclically. Sees "indirection, irony, and understatement" (211) as the source of the narration's success, much more appropriate to the purpose (he argues) than the sharp satire reviewer McCarthy desired.

Kilodney, Crad. "In Reply: In Defense of *The Handmaid's Tale*: A Rebuttal of Elizabeth Kingden's article (CCW Volume 10, No. 2)." *Cross-Canada Writers' Magazine* 11.1 (1989): 9, 32.

Argues that possibility, rather than probability, is the issue and that its relevance to current conditions is demonstrable.

Kingden, Elizabeth. "A Faulty Diagnosis of Society's Ills as Seen in Margaret Atwood's *The Handmaid's Tale*." *Cross-Canada Writers' Magazine* 10.2 (1988): 7, 32.

A birth-control activist, the reviewer is enraged by the premise of underpopulation and repulsed by a "sado-masochistic flavour to the detailed description of the enforced sexual act." Concedes it is literarily a "good read" but socially a dangerously false diagnosis and scoffs at the idea of "the world's greatest democracy [USA]" crumbling so easily.

Kizuk, A.R. "The Father's No and the Mother's Yes: Psychological Intertexts in Davies' *What's Bred in the Bone* and Atwood's *The Handmaid's Tale*." *Atlantis* 14.2 (Spring/printemps 1989): 1–9.

Sometimes interesting, often tortured comparison and readings of the two texts, with some errors and circular arguments.

Kolodny, Annette. "Margaret Atwood and the Politics of Narrative." *Studies on Canadian Literature: Introductory and Critical Essays*. Ed. Arnold E. Davidson. New York: MLA, 1990. 90–109.

Looks at Atwood's fiction from *The Edible Woman* through *The Handmaid's Tale*, detecting in Offred "the most anguished voice . . . to date, and the most self-conscious" (104). Declares the novel a warning against refusing political responsibility.

Kuester, Martin. "Atwood: Parodies from a Feminist Point of View." *Framing Truths: Parodic Structures in Contemporary English-Canadian Historical Novels*. Toronto: U of Toronto P, 1992. 124–52.

Chapter 5 looks at feminist parody in *Bodily Harm* and *The Handmaid's Tale*. Sees the *Tale* as paralleling, sometimes parodying, and reforming classic male dystopias, the Bible, U.S. slave narratives, canonical literature, and (via the "Historical Notes") historiography.

Lacombe, Michèle. "The Writing on the Wall: Amputated Speech in Margaret Atwood's *The Handmaid's Tale*." *Wascana Review* 21.2 (Fall 1986): 3–20.

Many controversial interpretations enliven this inquiry into language, imagery, symbolism, and sexual dynamics in the novel. Extremely gentle with the Commander and Pieixoto.

Langer, Beryl Donaldson. "Class and Gender in Margaret Atwood's Fiction." *Australian-Canadian Studies* 6.1 (1988): 73–101.

An excellent and thought-provoking article addressing class as the neglected factor in discussions of Atwood's fiction; sees the novel as spelling out some of the darker possibilities of our advanced capitalist culture. Defines Offred as one of Atwood's "new class" women, finally learning how fragile are the political gains of the last few decades.

Larson, Janet. "Margaret Atwood and the Future of Prophecy." *Religion & Literature* 21.1 (Spring 1989): 27–61.

Long article energetically tracing biblical parallels, rescriptings, and revisions in the novel, concerned to cast it as a new kind of prophecy in which the prophet (Offred) participates and is implicated.

___. "Margaret Atwood's Testaments: Resisting the Gilead Within." *Christian Century* 20–27 May 1987: 496–98.

Elaborates, with historical, biblical, and literary reference, Aunt Lydia's point that Gilead is within us, but also argues that resistance is everywhere possible.

Lehmann-Haupt, Christopher. "Books of the Times." *New York Times* 27 Jan. 1986: C24.

Praises the novel as Atwood's best to date, comparing her with several other current dystopian novelists and reviewing the strengths of the novel. Pursues its ambivalence toward villains en route to detecting a sadomasochistic fantasy operating in interesting tension with the political intent.

Linkous, Robert. "Margaret Atwood's *The Handmaid's Tale*." *San Francisco Review of Books* 11.3 (Fall 1986): 6.

Criticizes the novel's premise, plot, style, structure, pacing, and characterization, and compares it unfavourably with the "legitimately compelling, even terrifying" *Brave New World* and *Nineteen Eighty-Four*.

Lumsden, Charles. *Promethean Fire: Reflections on the Origin of the Mind*. Cambridge, MA: Harvard UP, 1983.

Source for a discarded epigraph; part of Atwood's background reading for the novel.

McCarthy, Mary. "Breeders, Wives and Unwomen." *New York Times Book Review* 9 Feb. 1986: 1, 35.

Negative early review by the famous novelist, finding weak characterization, "no satiric bite" (35), thin credibility, and a fatal lack of newspeak.

McCombs, Judith, and Carole L. Palmer. *Margaret Atwood: A Reference Guide*. Boston: Hall, 1991.

Meticulous annotated bibliography up to and including 1988, with succinct summaries of articles, reviews, and interviews.

McKie, David. "Communicating Futures: *The Handmaid's Tale* or *Terminator 2: Judgement Day*." *Australian Journal of Communication* 19.1 (1992): 1–8.

An article using the *Tale* as a facetious springboard to a call for environmentalism in Communications Studies.

Malak, Amin. "Margaret Atwood's 'The Handmaid's Tale' and the Dystopian Tradition." *Canadian Literature* 112 (Spring 1987): 9–16.

Studies the novel as a feminist dystopia in which the feminism is inclusive and ironic. Atwood is warning us that misogynous dogma, however innocent it appears at first, will with the addition of power become ruthless.

Marin, Richard T. "Among the Intellectualoids: Atwood at Work." *American Spectator* Jan. 1987: 35–37.

Caustic reviewer sees Atwood as missing "the slippery ambiguities" in her blunt vision of the sexes, and agrees with McCarthy that the novel lacks credibility and effective style and characterization.

Mathews, Laura. "A Fable for Our Times." *Glamour* Feb. 1986: 154.

Review praises the relevance, satiric wit, "probing, eloquent prose," deft avoidance of "bitter polemic" or straight "feminist nightmare." Applauds its "sure grasp of the consequences of moral rigidity and emotional passivity."

Miner, Madonne. " 'Trust me': Reading the Romance Plot in Margaret Atwood's *The Handmaid's Tale*." *Twentieth Century Literature* 37.2 (Summer 1991): 148–68.

An interest in wordplay and imagery informs this challenge to romantic readings of the novel, seeing Offred's affair with Nick as hackneyed true-romance thinking that perpetuates the social order.

Mollenkott, Virginia R. "A Tale of Two Handmaids." *Sensuous Spirituality: Out from Fundamentalism*. New York: Crossroad, 1992. 29–40.

Compares Offred and the Virgin Mary and exposes the misreading of biblical passages in aid of feminist Christianity and individual empowerment.

Murphy, Patrick D. "Reducing the Dystopian Distance: Pseudo-Documentary Framing in Near-Future Fiction." *Science-Fiction Studies* 17.1 (Mar. 1990): 25–40.

Criticizes at length Ketterer's article as wrongheadedly masculinist and argues that the novel's pseudo-documentary framing is a creative and effective twist to present a feminist dystopia in the clearly relevant near-future.

Nischik, Reingard M. "Back to the Future: Margaret Atwood's Anti-Utopian Vision in *The Handmaid's Tale*." *Englisch Amerikanische Studien* 9.1 (1987): 139–48.

Highly admiring article, defining Atwood's central intention as a warning against any sort of absolutist or despotic systems, in a scenario that shows the relation between general power structures or ideologies and the individual.

Norris, Ken. " 'The University of Denay, Nunavit': The 'Historical Notes' in Margaret Atwood's *The Handmaid's Tale*." *American Review of Canadian Studies* 20.3 (Autumn 1990): 357–64.

Systematic indictment of the conference of 2195 and its relationship with Offred's text. We, like Pieixoto, are implicated.

O'Brien, Tom. "Siren's Wail." *Commonweal* 25 Apr. 1986: 252.

Ambivalent review, valuing the novel as a well-executed warning, with humour, rich characterization, and action, but damaged by a very skimpy portrait of Gilead. Sees the novel as a regression from Atwood's developing creed against self-victimization.

Orwell, George. *Nineteen Eighty-Four*. New York: Harcourt, 1949.

A milestone dystopian novel about a future totalitarian state grimly dominated by slogans, by an official language called "Newspeak," and by compulsory worship of the leader, Big Brother. An ordinary man, Winston Smith, longs for better but eventually submits completely to the regime.

Parrinder, Patrick. "Making Poison." *London Review of Books* 20 Mar. 1986: 20–22.

Highly praising review, admiring the wordplay, humour, and sharp detail. Makes an interesting inquiry into the book as part of the allegedly ongoing Atwood premise that "fear is good for you" (20).

Peers, Elizabeth. "On Kilodney on Kingden on Atwood." Letter to the editor. *Cross-Canada Writers' Magazine* 11.3 (1989): 28.

Challenges Kilodney's factoring in authorial intentions and Kingden's expectations of social thesis and verisimilitude.

Piercy, Marge. *Woman on the Edge of Time*. New York: Fawcett, 1976.

Within the frame of a grimly realistic story about a woman in a contemporary New York mental institution, Piercy presents a utopian vision, an admirable future society free of sexism, racism, and ecological abuses.

"Questionnaire Results." Editorial. *Books in Canada* Aug.–Sept. 1990: 7.

Raschke, Debrah. "Margaret Atwood's *The Handmaid's Tale*: False Borders and Subtle Subversions." *Literature, Interpretation, Theory* 6.3–4 (1995): 257–68.

One of many articles on Atwood in this issue. Investigates three language systems: Gilead's, Offred's, and Pieixoto's.

Reesman, Jeanne Campbell. "Dark Knowledge in *The Handmaid's Tale*." CEA *Critic* 53.3 (Spring/Summer 1991): 6–22.

Argues Atwood's "profound feminist commitment [revealed] through language" (6) and sees the novel as marking "a sharp growth in Atwood's privileging of voice over vision" (11), tracing the ascendancy of dialogic over visual metaphors in the novel.

Roberson, Harriett. "Remembering Times to Come: Atwood Weaves Shocking Tale of Brutal Society." *Dallas Times Herald* 20 Apr. 1986: 12C.

Positive review of Atwood's "convincing and frightening" novel, described as a continuation of Atwood's interest in the female search for self and survival. Includes interesting play with name Serena Joy.

Rooke, Constance. "Atwood's Hands." *Fear of the Open Heart: Essays on Contemporary Canadian Writing*. Toronto: Coach House, 1989. 163–74.

Explores hands as a recurrent motif representing an alternate language, of gesture and touch.

___. "Interpreting *The Handmaid's Tale*: Offred's Name and 'The Arnolfini Marriage.' " *Fear of the Open Heart*. 175–96.

An essay that offers two types of interpretation: a systematic deciphering of Offred's coded name, June, and a freewheeling invocation of a well-known Flemish painting brought to mind by the convex mirror in the Commander's house.

Rosenberg, Jerome. "In a Future World, New Puritans Rule and Women Suffer." *Philadelphia Inquirer* 9 Feb. 1986: P1, P8.

Generally positive review, deeming the novel worthy of its dystopian predecessors. Comments especially upon style and finds flawed many passages of wooden, overly reflective prose and some gratuitous cleverness. Sees the "Historical Notes" as "delightful parody" and a useful gloss (P8).

Rosenthal, Pam. "The Future of Sexual Freedom." *Socialist Review* 87/88 (May/Aug. 1986): 151–56.

Highly praising review, identifying as core idea the belief that love can exist only between equals. Includes a sensible summary of dystopias and a lively reading of the text. Thinks the novel strong in its portrait of feminism and postfeminism but weak on antifeminism.

Rubenstein, Roberta. "Nature and Nurture in Dystopia: *The Handmaid's Tale*." VanSpanckeren and Castro 101–12.

A thematic study which shows Gilead's natural world completely denatured and nurturing obliterated in a system that objectifies, mutilates, and dismembers.

Rudy, Peter. Introduction. Zamiatin v–xi.

St. Peter, Christine. "Eye to I, Tail to Tale: Atwood, Offred and the Politicized Classroom." *Atlantis* 17.2 (Spring/Summer 1992): 93–103.

A strongly politicized essay arguing that Atwood and her text, both of them problematically feminist in their ambiguities, provide dynamic models of postmodern self-reflexivity, the hazards of complicity in patriarchy, and the falseness of an ideology of romantic love.

Sauterbailliet, Theresia. "*The Handmaid's Tale*." *Women's Studies International Forum* 14.3 (1991): 231–32.

A German review that applauds a new book trashing George Orwell's exclusionary male mystique, and then segues into Atwood's novel, which the reviewer finds politically and feministically astute and responsible.

Staines, David. "Dark Future of Today." *Dallas Morning News* 16 Mar. 1986: 10C.

Canadian reviewer sees the novel as a sharp commentary on our times and suggests that perhaps only a Canadian, "neighbor" but "outsider," "could create such an unsettling vision" of the U.S. future.

Stein, Karen F. "Margaret Atwood's *The Handmaid's Tale*: Scheherazade in Dystopia." *University of Toronto Quarterly* 61.2 (Winter 1991): 269–79.

Traces the multiple stories within the *Tale*, investigating problems of language, narrative, truth, and power.

Stimpson, Catharine R. "Atwood Woman." *The Nation* 31 May 1986: 764–67.

Lengthy review that calls Atwood one of "the most telling political writers in the West today" and celebrates the risky but successful interweaving of "the protest novel, the psychological novel and the bedroom farce" (764) in a feminist dystopia that it would be hazardous to ignore.

Sussman, Vic. "She-Devils and Handmaidens." Rev. of audio book. *Book World* [*Washington Post*] 23 Dec. 1990: 8.

One of the third wave of reviews, the first following the hardcover publication, the second after the paperback appeared, and the third after the unabridged audiocassettes and film version arrived. This reviewer is so impressed that he recommends similar recordings (now available) of *Cat's Eye* and *Bluebeard's Egg*.

Thomas, Gillian. "Atwood's Novel Vision." *Atlantic Provinces Book Review* 12.4 (Nov.–Dec. 1985): 26.

Ambivalent review, challenging details in the novel but convinced of the plausibility and impressed with the subtle probing of sexual politics. Sees the "Historical Notes" as showing the same old sexism and pedantry as exist now.

Thompson, James J., Jr. "Bashing the Bible-Thumpers." *The World & I* 1.5 (May 1986): 438–42.

Denounces in detail Atwood's grasp of fundamentalism and her fictional rendering thereof.

Thurman, Judith. "When You Wish upon a Star." *New Yorker* 29 May 1989: 108–10.

A review of *Cat's Eye* that discusses *The Handmaid's Tale* and argues that while the latter "wasn't plausible psychologically or politically, it *was* plausible as a metaphor of incest and a fantasy of bondage," a direction primly undeveloped by Atwood.

Tilley, Nancy. "Margaret Atwood's Tale of Freedom Lost." *News and Observer* [Raleigh, NC] 2 Mar. 1986: C8–C9.

A positive review, reading "desperation" between the lines, and calling the novel a "riveting" and "passionate" "parable about the fragility of human happiness" within a portrait of "a world . . . of female domination and female powerlessness," in which "we are all implicated."

Tomc, Sandra. " 'The Missionary Position': Feminism and Nationalism in Margaret Atwood's *The Handmaid's Tale*." *Canadian Literature* 138/139 (Fall/Winter 1993): 73–87.

Queries the novel's reception as feminist, but circles around to argue that Atwood's use of passivity, low (female) cultural artifacts, and sentimental romance are Canadian resistances to an American/Puritan tradition of action, control, rationalism.

Tyler, Anne. "Margaret Atwood's Chilling New Tale of a Future America." *Chicago Sun-Times* 2 Feb. 1986: 28.

Famous novelist admires the immediacy, suspense, great detail, and relevance to our times. Her only reservation is the way the "Historical Notes" cast the tale into the past, interfering with the sense of immediacy achieved by Offred's use of present tense.

Updike, John. "Expeditions to Gilead and Seegard." *New Yorker* 12 May 1986: 118–23.

Another famous novelist weighs in with a long, fascinating review praising the poet and the Canadianness in Atwood that made possible this "quizzi- cal, delicate, and ultimately moving" leap of the imagination. Reflects that "To Canadians we must seem a violent and somewhat sinister nation. . . . [Canada] stands above, as it were, much of our moral strenuousness, our noisy determination to combine virtue and power, and our occasional vast miscarriages of missionary intention" (118).

VanSpanckeren, Kathryn, and Jan Garden Castro, eds. *Margaret Atwood: Vision and Forms*. Carbondale: Southern Illinois UP, 1988.

Wain, Alan. Letter to the editor. *Cross-Canada Writers' Magazine* 11.3 (1989): 28.

Points out contradictions in Kilodney's defence of Atwood against Kingden's criticisms.

Warner, Marina. "Stepford Revisited." *London Guardian* 20 Mar. 1986: 20.

Negative review, deploring the way people "come second" in Atwood's dystopia, and describing Offred as a "flattened" character, "distanced by the prose," with Luke and Nick mere "shadows."

Waugh, Harriet. "Love and Death at Sea." *Illustrated London News* 274 (May 1986): 90–91.

Ambivalent British review, both admiring the way Atwood "brilliantly conveys the horror and boredom of captivity" and lamenting the lack of "real excitement" (91), the minimalist plot, and the paradox that the book was fascinating and yet not pleasurable to read. Sees Gilead as already existing on our globe and applauds the warning that freedom can easily be taken away.

Wilson, Sharon Rose. *Margaret Atwood's Fairy-Tale Sexual Politics*. Jackson: UP of Mississippi, 1993.

Chapter 10, "Off the Path to Grandma's House in *The Handmaid's Tale*," explores the novel as an "anti-narrative that both comments on and undercuts its varied intertexts, especially the fairy tale" (271), and our reading practices and theories as well.

Wood, Diane S. "Bradbury and Atwood: Exile as Rational Decision." *The Literature of Emigration and Exile*. Ed. James Whitlark and Wendell Aycock. *Studies in Comparative Literature* 23. Lubbock: Texas Tech UP, 1992. 131–42.

Sees both writers and their texts as concerned with the gradual erosion and loss of freedoms, the critical role of words and reading in resisting that loss, and the complicity of the population involved.

Workman, Nancy V. "Sufi Mysticism in Margaret Atwood's *The Handmaid's Tale*." *Studies in Canadian Literature* 14.2 (1989): 10–26.

Sees the Sufi epigraph to the novel as a unifying element, and details the parallels between Sufism and Offred.

Zamiatin, Eugene. *We*. 1920. Trans. Gregory Zilboorg. Introd. Peter Rudy. New York: Dutton, 1959.

A bitter dystopian classic of Soviet literature, considered the inspiration for George Orwell's *Nineteen Eighty-Four*. Zamiatin's definition of a good book is cited by Rudy in the introduction.

Updated checklists of Atwood scholarship are published annually in the *Newsletter of the Margaret Atwood Society*. The most recent of these was compiled by Ashley Thomson and Danette DiMarco for 1995 (No. 16, Spring/Summer 1996). The *Newsletter* is edited by Jerome Rosenberg, English Department, Miami University, Oxford, Ohio 45056, Facsimile: (513) 529-1392, E-mail: Rosenberg_Jerome@msmail.muohio.edu.

Index